STEINER'S THEOSOPHY
&
PRINCIPLES OF SPIRITUAL SCIENCE

ALSO BY CARL UNGER

The Language of the Consciousness Soul
A Guide to Rudolf Steiner's "Leading Thoughts"
(SteinerBooks, 2012)

Steiner's Theosophy
&
Principles of
Spiritual Science

Carl Unger

STEINERBOOKS | 2014

2014
SteinerBooks
An imprint of Anthroposophic Press, Inc.
610 Main St., Great Barrington, MA 01230
www.steinerbooks.org

Copyright © 2014 by Anthroposophic Press, Inc. All rights reserved. No part of this publication may be reproduced, stored in a retrieval system, or transmitted, in any form or by any means, electronic, mechanical, photocopying, recording, or otherwise, without the prior written permission of the publisher.

Library of Congress Control Number: 2014933230

ISBN: 978-1-62148-061-7 (paperback)
ISBN: 978-1-62148-062-4 (ebook)

Contents

Editorial Note		vii
PART ONE: NOTES ON RUDOLF STEINER'S BOOK *THEOSOPHY*		1
	Introduction	3
1.	Genuine Spiritual Science Based on Steiner's Theosophy	11
2.	Spiritual Teacher and Learner	17
3.	The Essential Nature of the Human Being	25
4.	Body, Soul, and Spirit	31
5.	Manas, Budhi, and Atma	35
6.	Re-embodiment of the Spirit and Destiny	41
7.	Perceiving in the Soul World	47
8.	Sensory Observation, Thinking, and Cognition	51
PART TWO: PRINCIPLES OF SPIRITUAL SCIENCE		53
1.	The "I" and the Nature of the Human Being	55
2.	Natural Science and Spiritual Science	77
3.	The Philosophy of Contradiction	99

Editorial Note

Carl Unger spoke about Rudolf Steiner's book *Theosophy* in about sixty anthroposophic meetings in 1908 and 1909. His carefully prepared notes, which form the first part of this book, were intended as a framework for those talks, which covered approximately the first half of *Theosophy*

The following brief biography is based on a paper written by Carl Unger for Marie Steiner around 1925, describing the anthroposophic work in Stuttgart and offering autobiographical statements.

Carl Theodor Unger was born on March 28, 1878, in Cannstatt near Stuttgart. He belonged to the family of a merchant with a scientific background. His grandfather, E. S. Unger, was Professor of Mathematics at the University of Erfurt and the founder of the first German Secondary School (*Realschule*). His father, J. Unger, was known as a collector of art.

As a child Carl Unger was distinguished for his musical ability and above all for his early interest in philosophy as well as for his scientific and technological talents. He received a secular education, and, from the age of fourteen on, he often visited the home of Adolf Arenson. The impressions those visits had on him were very important for his life. Although there was a difference of twenty-three years of age, he and Arenson developed a deep friendship. When he was fifteen years old, Carl Unger was very impressed with Kerner's *Seer of Prevorat*—primarily by the objectivity of the book in terms of suprasensory experiences, which caused his "childish materialism" to fade away.

When he reached seventeen, he asked Adolf Arenson about his view of the world. The question was almost unexpected. His friend presented him with the doctrine of reincarnation, "which, when extricating himself from spiritualistic experiences, he had already discovered for himself, and had found confirmed by Lessing." After that, this also became Unger's view.

He attended the humanistic *Gymnasium*, or high school, which includes classes in Latin and Greek. Later, he attended technical colleges in Stuttgart and Berlin-Charlottenburg and "took the usual examinations." He had studied mechanics and attained his diploma in engineering, as well as a PhD.

At the age of twenty, Unger's destiny brought him a strange interruption. During his military service—due to an unfortunate joke—he was shot by a comrade with a pistol, which, of course, was thought to be unloaded. The bullet went into his pericardium (the tissue surrounding the heart). For a long time he hovered between life and death, and it never became possible to remove the bullet. This experience made him conscious that his life had been given to him afresh by the spiritual world, and that it should be devoted to serving that world.[1]

Shortly before the twentieth century, during a conversation with an artist friend about reincarnation, Unger and Arenson were introduced to the Theosophical Society. They became members in 1902, when Rudolf Steiner was General Secretary of the German section of that society. In the

---

[1] See study 24 in Carl Unger, *The Language of the Consciousness Soul: A Guide to Rudolf Steiner's "Leading Thoughts"* (SteinerBooks, 2012).

autumn of the following year, Arenson, who was the first to become acquainted with Steiner, returned to Stuttgart deeply impressed by what he had heard in Berlin; but his impressions were received with skepticism.

By February 1904, Unger also wished to meet with Steiner in Berlin to express, among other things, the wish that more might be known of the society's German section. He describes this meeting:

> At the time, I had still not read one line by Dr. Steiner. On the occasion of this first conversation he was very silent, but he took me to Mrs. van Sivers, who, in his presence, pointed to the necessity of beginning the lecture journey, which had been long intended—especially now that Dr. Steiner's book *Theosophy* was ready to be published. Mrs. von Sivers invited me to a lecture by Dr. Steiner, which was to occur that evening; the lecture was on the passage from the Creed, "suffered under Pontius Pilate." This lecture immediately convinced me that this was a man to whose work I must dedicate my life. The strongest impression was this: Here is one who sees and knows.
>
> When I returned to Stuttgart, my enthusiasm was received, as was Mr. Arenson's, with skepticism. Some months later, Dr. Steiner began his lecture tours. Meanwhile, his book *Theosophy* was published, and I threw myself into it with the greatest enthusiasm, wrestling with it for months with every page, every sentence, and many words. When I had the foundation for a judgment, which I had somewhat carelessly expressed after my visit to Berlin, I would follow this man blindfolded. For now I had learned to follow with open eyes.[2]

---

[2] From a paper written by Carl Unger for Marie Steiner around 1925, describing the anthroposophic work in Stuttgart (unpublished in English).

The time had come to focus the activity of the Stuttgart Group in terms of the work indicated by Rudolf Steiner. Unger made a proposal that was not carried; so he, Arenson, and some other friends resigned from that group to begin a new one on September 23, 1905. The intention of this work was, "through the experience of thinking, to go deeply into the human being and into the being of the world in order to encounter the Spiritual Science of Rudolf Steiner with a suitable activity." After 1905, Unger was a personal pupil of Rudolf Steiner.

In 1907, at Steiner's instigation, Unger presented a lecture at the Congress of the European sections of the Theosophical Society in Munich on the work accomplished by the Stuttgart group. As a result of this lecture, invitations came from numerous groups. Consequently, between 1907 and 1913, he gave hundreds of lectures to many groups in Germany and Switzerland.

This was made possible in this way: in the fall of 1906, with the help of his father, he had established a small machine factory with a definite intention of becoming completely independent. "This brought in its wake many business difficulties, but it also offered me the opportunity of an outer and, even more, an inner freedom. Indeed, I also gained some experience of life as a result of this."

That year brought him—immediately following his marriage to one of Arenson's daughters—another important conversation with Rudolf Steiner, who advised him to work in the realm of epistemology. This led to some writings that have appeared in part as books and articles. From that time on, Unger continued to work along those lines.

The Anthroposophical Society, founded in 1912, required an administrative body after 1913. Unger was then thirty-five and had belonged to its council from the beginning. In

Editorial Note

1914, another task was added when Steiner—regretfully, as he said—was obliged to accept Unger's offer to oversee the work of building the Goetheanum, though it was also "anticipated that this would mean a loss to the work in the Society." It was possible only to continue this work until September 1915. After that, war conditions prevented journeys into Switzerland.

During the period immediately after World War I, Unger, together with others, devoted his strength to the many tasks that fell to the anthroposophic movement in every area of life. He paid particular attention, however, to the actual impulses of the Anthroposophical Society, while many became less conscious of them. This was owing to the necessity arising from Anthroposophy to work in the world in general—in education, medicine, and so on. His particular work during the last years of his life was his writing in relation to studying Steiner's leading thoughts.

Unger, however, was not simply a lecturer and independent worker in the Anthroposophical Society. When Der Kommender Tag was founded, there was an attempt, after World War I, to apply the ideas of the Threefold Social Order. Unger made his factory a part of that enterprise. When the enterprise failed, however, he was again obliged to assume independent ownership of his factory. This meant accepting the burden involved in an effort that proved a failure.

In the final years of his life, Unger toured to lecture publicly in addition to his work in the Society. On January 4, 1929, in Nuremberg, immediately before a lecture on one such tour, a bullet overtook him—this time fatal—for which an irresponsible person was the tool. The title of the lecture was "What Is Anthroposophy?"

PART ONE

Notes on Rudolf Steiner's Book *Theosophy*

Introduction

The age that began with the publication of Kant's *Critique of Pure Reason* may be called, with certain justification, the "age of criticism." Criticism and doubt have insinuated themselves into all the realms of our life, even to the very depths of the soul. Certainly, doubt is a familiar phenomenon in human history, but in terms of the fundamental problems of life there has scarcely been a period of time when there was so little security and certitude as there is in our own. Not only have the tremendous achievements in the knowledge and mastery of nature not improved this condition, they have actually caused the eye of the spirit to fixate on outer phenomena in expectation of a solution to the mysteries of the soul from that direction. Although it is clear that such observation of outer facts in relation to the soul life has failed entirely, today's consciousness has nonetheless become so anxious in the face of so-called subjective facts of the soul[1] that we are left with little but weary resignation. Such fearfulness over so-called mere subjective results has gripped thinking to the extent that confidence in thinking has all but disappeared.

---

1 As in many forms of psychoanalysis. —ED.

Nevertheless, every sentence that claims to shatter confidence in thinking expresses an unconscious recognition of thinking. Certainly, any discussion of thinking as a mere process in the brain has long been recognized to be impossible. Moreover, it is also realized that absolute skepticism speaks against itself in every sentence it speaks; but to move on from this perspective to actual confidence in thinking still requires a long journey. Yet we may say that the appearance of doubt shows that the reality of knowledge is being attested and sought in this way. In the actual process of following our doubt we activate our confidence in thinking, whereas doubt—when developed into a method—is simply a theory of knowledge.

It may seem bold in our time when, in relation to Anthroposophy, or Spiritual Science, we now speak of confidence in thinking. True, it might be supposed that we must renounce all thinking of our own if we acknowledge the teachings of Spiritual Science. Moreover, certain self-styled theosophical circles and individuals consider themselves justified in viewing all thinking and science with contempt from their perspective of supposed spiritual experience. Indeed, an exposition of true Spiritual Science is needed today because so much charlatanism and fraud parade themselves in the area of esotericism. However, even what is written by brilliant contemporaries about Spiritual Science and *Theosophy* does not induce the reader to expect from Spiritual Science very much that would contribute to the satisfaction of philosophical needs. Isn't it possible, however, that such judgments may be attributed to the fact that such writers have not considered it worth their while, with all the keenness of their reason, to enter the teachings of Spiritual Science more deeply? Could it be that they have not done what the author of *Theosophy* declared in his preface about this task: "In some respects, its readers will have to work their way through each page and even each single sentence the hard way" (p. 8).[2]

Only one example will be given here to illustrate the attitude of today's best minds in the presence of the weightiest world problems. Maurice Maeterlinck[3] writes in his book *Death:*

> The God who offers us the best and mightiest religion has given us our intellect so that we may use it honestly and without restriction—that is, to strive most of all and in all circumstances toward what appears as truth to our reason. Can this God demand that, contrary to our reason, we swear allegiance to a faith whose incertitude is admitted even by its most zealous and keenest champions?

And two sentences later:

> Three hundred years of apologetics have been unable to add one tenable item of evidence to this terrible despairing point of view of Pascal. This, then, is all that the human intellect has discovered to compel us to belief. If the God who demands belief from us does not wish us to guide ourselves through our intellect, then how can we choose?

Here Maeterlinck demands the most unrestricted and conscientious use of the intellect. How are we to explain the fact

---

[2] Carl Unger refers mainly to the first German edition of *Theosophy*. Page numbers in this edition refer to the English edition translated by Catherine E. Creeger from the 19th German revised edition and published in 1994 by Anthroposophic Press. Rudolf Steiner continued to revise and amend *Theosophy* through its 9th edition.

[3] Maurice Maeterlinck (1862–1949) was a Belgian playwright, poet, and essayist who wrote in French. He was awarded the Nobel Prize in Literature in 1911. The main themes in his work are death and the meaning of life. His plays form an important part of the Symbolist movement.

that he is wholly ignorant of the most important material bearing upon *Theosophy*, to which he devotes two whole pages of his book? What he presents is twenty or thirty years out of date. In the course of his reflections, however, it is clear, too, that although he does indeed demand the use of reason, he has such little confidence in thinking that he knows scarcely any other use of reason except what corresponds more or less to everyday thinking. He fails to see that thinking must adapt to the new realm that is to be revealed, and that it is out of order to demand proofs that corroborate the suprasensory in a way that applies to sensory phenomena.

This book endeavors to present to the public what may be experienced in connection with the book *Theosophy* by a form of thinking that has trained itself to the utmost keenness of criticism. The intellectual confirmation of a spiritual doctrine has always been called an apologia. However, because the more recent apologetic literature consists mostly of refuting criticisms brought against a worldview or a religion, very little is thus achieved toward the actual corroboration of such a worldview itself. Therefore, we will undertake a more positively apologetic study to show how the teachings of Spiritual Science, as expounded by Rudolf Steiner, can stand the test of the rational consciousness.

Steiner himself emphatically declares again and again that it is possible, with a little goodwill, to grasp rationally all the teachings he has presented; but this is something that must actually be done. It will become clear in the book itself why Steiner himself only suggests the solution to this problem. However, if an audience simply appeals to his assertion, nothing is achieved. Once we set ourselves to the task of "working it over" it certainly becomes evident that, to grasp Spiritual Science rationally, reason itself must first be educated in many things. Is it, then, entirely certain that we already know, from ordinary life, what the capacities of reason are? Hasn't reason already accomplished great achievements in newly mastered areas?

Let us convince ourselves through an area that seems very remote. The axioms of geometry, as laid down by Euclid, have remained unmodified for centuries as the basic definitions of space. Only recently has critical thinking begun to doubt whether all these axioms were needed to pursue geometry; for example, it has been possible to drop Euclid's axiom of parallel lines. Without this, we can develop a science of geometry, but we have to conceive the space to which it applies in a different way. In connection with such scientific research associated with the names of Lobachevsky, Bolyai, Riemann,[4] and others, the question has often been raised as to which science of geometry corresponds to reality, or how actual space must be viewed. Once we grasp such research from the point of view of their significance for the use of reason, we will find that in such endeavors reason long ago passed beyond the limits Kant believed he could set for it.

In the real sense of a theory of knowledge, thinking itself has set the most rigid limits, declaring logic to be absolute in disregarding the fact that logic must actually follow the requirements of cognition. The needs of a theory of cognition and their logical evaluation first appear, even historically, only after a certain accumulation of knowledge has developed in the corresponding field. New elements of knowledge force their

---

4   Nikolai Lobachevsky (1792–1856), Russian mathematician and geometer; János Bolyai (1802–1860), Hungarian mathematician; Bernhard Riemann (1826–1866), German mathematician.

way through, even against dominant logical formulas of a theory of cognition.

Yet, even until a very recent period, the basic principle of contradiction as formulated by Aristotle continued to exert its determinative influence. The appearance of a contradiction in scientific thinking was not questioned as evidence of a fallacy; one tried to refute an opinion by showing that it contains contradictions or leads to contradictions. Hegel came into a conflict with this view when he proposed contradiction as an element of cognition. The fact that the time simply passed over Hegel may one day be considered proof of his extraordinary significance; perhaps, however, even today we may see evidence of possible reason in the fact that a profound thinker appeared at that time whose thinking was able to endure contradiction and thus recognize it as a solution to the mystery of knowledge. Doesn't it seem as though, with Hegel, philosophy cried out for the results of a new kind of knowledge, whose experiences, being suprasensory, must contradict ordinary sensory experience?

The fact that contradiction now appears in the presence of the basic questions of knowledge, as Kant pointed out in principle, should not lead to the absurd notion that there is no such thing as true, or "objective," knowledge. It may be acknowledged that—in the presence of the basic questions of knowledge as formulated today—every answer indicates a contradiction. Nevertheless, the reason for this may lay in a false evaluation of the basic question itself. The basic principle of contradiction—owing to which knowledge may be denied—is derived from reason itself, which is supposed to be dethroned by such a judgment.

Introduction

The essential question of knowledge can be expressed briefly: Can the thing be for me as it is in itself? If nothing but an affirmative answer to this question can be considered knowledge, then every item of knowledge must appear to be a contradiction. Yet one thing that is for me "as it is in itself" answers this question immediately: the "I," which appears here as the father of all contradictions. The formulation of the basic question of knowledge shows that the "I" sees itself as separate from the "world." However, the "I" is not justified in itself to draw the limits of the principle of contradiction. Indeed, we may say: The "I," by forming the basic question, expresses the fact that its whole being is an expression of the sensory perspective and shows in itself a living contradiction in the presence of the true reality, and it expresses the fact that attempting to bridge the chasm between "I" and the world is evidence of the fact that our true being must seek its reality in the suprasensory. If the perspective of the sensory is thus a contradiction against true reality, all answers to the basic question of knowledge that may appear as contradictions would really be contradictions against the contradiction. In this way, we could overcome the unconditional validity of the principle of contradiction and reveal a path to recognizing the suprasensory. Nevertheless, we will quickly discover that logical disclosure of the suprasensory does not lead to positive results, but only to generalities and, finally, to arguments opposed to arguments.

It is entirely different, however, when a suprasensory fact appears with positive experiential results. Then, based on these reflections, we have ample reason to occupy ourselves with these results, because we will then be prepared to consider them with reason that learns through these results without being sidetracked by general opposing arguments. We will then certainly not argue against the possibility of such results for those who do not know the results of suprasensory research and do not wish to learn them. However, perhaps we will be able to learn that genuine and earnest Spiritual Science answers to the cry that philosophy sends forth from its whole past.[5]

---

[5] Carl Unger notes at this point his concern that this book should not be a substitute for reading Rudolf Steiner's book *Theosophy:*

> There is something dubious in the thought of writing a book about a book. The book has been widely read. Obviously, the book can be read only in the actual work itself. We must avoid detracting from the original through our commentary. Respect for the documents will not be diminished through our understanding of them.

1

Genuine Spiritual Science Based on Steiner's Theosophy

> *"This book cannot be read the way people ordinarily read books in this day and age. In some respects, its readers will have to work their way through each page and even each single sentence the hard way."*
> —Rudolf Steiner, preface to Theosophy (p. 7)

These sentences are an impressive passport for us when we decide to occupy ourselves with the book *Theosophy: An Introduction to the Spiritual Processes in Human Life and in the Cosmos*.[1] Every reader of *Theosophy* will have the experience that it reveals its content only gradually. Moreover, it is certain that readers will bring to the book itself the results of each new understanding through their own efforts. It is in the very nature of the work that it is necessary, first, to permit a book that presents a certain worldview to work upon us without preconceptions, even though it may be very difficult for many today to gain freedom from bias, specifically in the case of a book that proposes to introduce realms of the suprasensory.

---

1 When *Theosophy* was written in 1904, Rudolf Steiner headed the German section of the Theosophical Society. Later, when he began using the term *Anthroposophy*, he let it be known that *Theosophy* and *Anthroposophy* were synonymous in regard to his teaching.

However, after the first unbiased study of *Theosophy*, when we apply ourselves repeatedly to experiencing its truths, it must follow that we cease to be without preconceptions about those passages that have become true "experience" (in the sense conveyed by the writer), since those very passages will form the basis for further penetration into the book. We will win from the book itself, little by little, the point of view for judging it. This will always be the case, and not just for the prevailing scientific mode of examination, which the author explicitly declares necessary. Thus, we will sometimes return to the first sentences and pages with the content of the whole book in our consciousness, and we will find that the very preface and introduction speak to us with a special intimacy when we consider them under the influence of the whole work.

Such a consideration of the preface and the introduction will be sought in what follows. Indeed, we may say in general that, in the case of most books, the preface and the introduction are written after the essential content of the book itself has been composed, so that we can demonstrate the influence of the book itself on its preface and introduction—especially since such an influence is mostly produced purposely. In the preface we generally discover the relationship between the author and the book, and in an introduction, the relationship that the author expects of the reader. Such perspectives may be of importance to the reader of a book dealing with a worldview and proposing to introduce us into the suprasensory world! Won't readers who have been serious in "mastering by their own effort" be able to find a picture of their own process of becoming if they try to evoke the content of the whole book from the preface and introduction? In this case, the following may develop.

In the first sentences of the preface, the author of the book *Theosophy* confronts readers with a decision that they must make themselves. Some readers may be among those "believing only in the validity of the sense-perceptible world" (p. 7). This book, then, was not written for them. Alternatively, they may be "interested in finding pathways leading out of the sense-perceptible world" (ibid.). In any case, the reader must ask: Do I wish to look for the ways that lead out of the sensory world? We can see that much self-assessment is needed to answer such a question. Perhaps the reader will test this question in a general way by the one case now confronting her or him, and will ask: What induces me to read a book that, even in its title, refers to the suprasensory? In an honest self-examination, one will not be permanently satisfied by pointing to external, perhaps seemingly accidental, inducements. However, if we really seek to penetrate through all the details of life to the deeper foundations of our inner nature, every reader will find that, in the final analysis, it comes to light that we are really "interested in finding pathways leading out of the sense-perceptible world." It can actually be proven that this fact faces everyone who performs such self-examination.

We need to look into our own inner being if we are to find the motives and true causes that have impelled us. In other words, we turn our eyes away from the sensory to the suprasensory that lives and weaves in our own inner being. It may well be, however, that the author of this book wishes to bring readers face to face with their own initial relationship to the suprasensory by holding up a mirror to them and allowing them to decide whether or not to look into it. Readers who look into their own inner being already seek "pathways leading out of the sense-perceptible world." Moreover, if readers perhaps feel a certain terror when they read the word *suprasensory*, even in the title and in the first sentence, they may take some comfort when directed to an aspect of the suprasensory with which one ought to be at least somewhat acquainted.

This first form of the suprasensory that the author introduces to the reader demands that we avert our eyes from the "effects" (for example, from reading the book) and come to know the "causes." Thus, what follows suggests a suprasensory fact: "It is only through knowledge of the suprasensory that our sense-perceptible 'reality' acquires meaning" (p. 8). It cannot be doubted that the transition from effects to causes is something truly practical; those who look into their own inner being will not only find that the question of life's value and meaning resounds within us—that is, in the suprasensory—but also that the motives for "practical" action must flow from within.

If we thus see how, under the stimulus to self-examination, the beginning of the preface seems to flow from the reader's inner being, nothing can hinder us from moving forward in the same spirit through further studies.

Thus we have become acquainted with a suprasensory fact that may play a role in the reader, and it will therefore not be so repellent if the author of the book speaks in his own way about suprasensory facts; to "testify...on the basis of personal experience in this field" (ibid.) shows that the author will report facts. However, to gain a relationship to the suprasensory facts that the author will present (which signify something other than the suprasensory facts that readers find within themselves), "readers will have to work their way through each page and even each single sentence the hard way.... The spiritual-scientific truths it [the book] contains must be experienced" (ibid.). Accordingly, what is reported as suprasensory facts should be experienced by the reader as truth. Here, the content of the book itself must be considered if we want to grasp correctly what is meant by experience.

It would be easy to think that here the author demands that the reader must experience the suprasensory facts in the same way as the author himself experienced them. We could, perhaps, point to the last chapter, "The Path to Knowledge," and say that the content of such a book has real value only when we ourselves have traveled the path to knowledge and gained a view for ourselves into the suprasensory worlds. Certainly "mastery by our own effort"[2] is finally to gain a relationship with the path to knowledge; but it would be strange if the whole book were able to gain value only from its final chapter. The author cannot, in the preface, wish to make a demand of the reader if the way to fulfil such a demand were indicated only in the final chapter. There must surely be another way to experience suprasensory facts as truth. This other way, then, must be sought in the book itself; it may well come to light that this other way of experiencing suprasensory facts as truth must be practiced, because it provides the prerequisite condition on which we may seek the kind of experience discussed in the final chapter.

The shift of our attention from effects to causes, however, has still further significance. When we seek the causes of certain effects given to us as facts, this is the truly scientific perspective, which should "not be contradicted at all" in the author's exposition. Thus in the book itself we may observe how the genuinely scientific spirit is to relate itself to facts. In

---

2 See *Theosophy*, chapter 4: "Anyone who scorns strenuous mental effort as a way of acquiring higher knowledge, turning instead to other forces available to us, is not taking into account the fact that thinking is the highest of the faculties we human beings possess in the physical world" (p. 176).

addition, we will be led even further by reflecting on the relationship between facts that confront us as effects and their causes, which we should seek in a genuinely scientific spirit. Assuming that certain facts confront us in any area, a truly scientific spirit will view these as effects and look for their causes. It will come to light that these causes, when discovered as facts, may be viewed in turn as effects of other causes, so that scientific research advances from cause to cause, from question to question. This is a course that, as a scientific endeavor, moves in the direction opposite to the course of the evolution of phenomena. If we consider the course of world evolution as a progressive advance in time, scientific research must move backward in time to reach the primal foundation of existence. It becomes appropriate to direct scientific research toward the future only when a certain "elementary level" has been found in a given area. However, at every stage the question to be asked can arise only from the next preceding answer. In other words, "Only through understanding these elementary stages can we learn how to ask questions of a higher sort" (p. 9).

Thus, the whole content of the preface, as presented in the first edition of the book, may take its form from a self-examination of the reader's own inner nature. Our studies mostly follow the text of the first edition, although there will be occasion to avail ourselves of the substance of added passages in later editions. It is possible to gain a special relationship to these expansions and comments once we succeed in showing that they may be found in essence between the lines of the first edition. In such supplementary passages we can find a confirmation for many results of "mastery by our own effort" and an aid to deepening ourselves further in the book's content.

2

Spiritual Teacher and Learner

Once we realize that the content of the introduction seems to press upon us only from without—as a stimulant to self-examination—but that the individual paragraphs represent facts of our own inner nature, existent and needing only to have our attention directed to them, this may become a matter of great significance for us. First, readers may actually experience, even in the preface, the power of the book to awaken; it addresses a challenge to our inner nature, and we will be able to decide to entrust ourselves to the guidance of the author, who writes in the preface only what may resound in the inner nature of readers themselves and every individual human being. Readers thus find themselves in agreement with their own inner being, and this sense of agreement indicates a feeling of their own freedom in relation to the book. It is this that is especially expressed in the preface; not only will it grant the fullest freedom to the readers, but it will actually create this for them. Thus the reference to the author's *Philosophy of Spiritual Activity*[1] appears in a special light.

---

1   *Die Philosophie der Freiheit* (1894); published in English under several titles, including *Intuitive Thinking as a Spiritual Path: A Philosophy of Freedom* (Collected Works [CW], vol. 4). All following references are to that translation.

In *The Philosophy of Spiritual Activity,* chapter 1, (intended as a preface), rather than Fichte's intention in *An Attempt to Force the Reader to Understand,*[2] we find: "Today no one should be compelled to understand. We demand neither recognition nor agreement from those who are not driven to a given opinion by their own particular, individual needs" (pp. 254–255). This mood, to which *The Philosophy of Spiritual Activity* is dedicated, we find beautifully exemplified in the preface to the book we are now considering. When the author therefore promises, as it were, in the preface to respect the reader's freedom, likewise the reader may respond by assuming an attitude that one "no longer needs to be compelled to understand, but wants to understand" (p. 255).

If the preface has thus become something belonging inwardly to us personally, a glance at the preface as a whole will show that we must consider what has occurred within us. As we thus take a general survey, we will be impressed by the fact that each paragraph confronts us with contrasts—sensory and suprasensory; cause and effect; the author's experience and the reader's experience; ordinary reading and reading in this case; ordinary science and true science; philosophy and theosophy; and ultimate truth and initial questioning. It is useful to assume a view with reference to such contrasts. We feel soul needs inwardly stimulated that may have thus far been asleep, but that now show that we are individuals who seek ways out of the sensory world. When the soul senses such contrasts, we aspire for knowledge. Indeed the author desires to meet such an aspiration, but he can do so only when readers themselves

---

2 J. G. Fichte, *A Crystal Clear Report to the General Public Concerning the Actual Essence of the Newest Philosophy: An Attempt to Force the Reader to Understand, in Philosophy of German Idealism* (London: Bloomsbury, 1987).

show that they in need of new cognition. Readers whose inner nature responds to the challenge of the author will understand "that cultivation of suprasensory knowledge is a necessity of our time" (p. 9). The fact, however, that the contrasts mentioned are indeed present indicates that contemporary habits of thought bring it to pass that "what many people nowadays reject most emphatically is precisely what they most urgently need" (p. 10). The earnestly aspiring will feel impelled to revise their habits of thought.

Such are the reflections dealt with in the supplemental passages of the preface in later editions. To see clearly the demands that readers may make on themselves through their own decision, through inner freedom, we must place ourselves at the central point of the preface, where such demands appear, and from there must take our own survey.

"The truths of the book must be experienced." To this end the mastery through the reader's own efforts must contribute. However, what should be experienced as truth consists of suprasensory facts, which should come to the reader as something new compared to what one already recognizes as suprasensory through self-examination. What is meant by the experience of a truth? Are we, then, already capable of experiencing sensory facts as truth? Certainly, this is the purpose of "the genuine scientific spirit." Nonetheless, we must look for an answer to the question inherent in a theory of knowledge: How are facts experienced as truth? We then come to know the reverse question, which is so important for the true conduct of life—indeed, a question dealt with in an independent way in *The Philosophy of Spiritual Activity*: How should truths we experience be transformed into facts?[3]

---

3 See *Intuitive Knowledge as a Spiritual Path*, ch. 2, pp. 18ff.

A survey of the preface of *Theosophy* shows that it is necessary to gain a perspective in relation to two requirements and that everything else is connected with this. First, we should establish inner clarity within ourselves as to the way that the author offers suprasensory facts—how the author should be distinguished from a scientist who investigates sensory facts. Second, we ourselves must clearly understand the significance of experiencing facts as truth.

We will see how the author gradually meets these requirements. Karl Rosenkranz, in his book *Logic*,[4] devotes a brief paragraph to "hermeneutics," the art of interpretation. He writes, "The interpreter must in a reproduction, once more, as it were, create the thing itself. Here is expressed an ideal not easily attained. However, even to approach this ideal it will be necessary that the 'hermeneutics' shall first have actually attained by one's own effort to the very kernel of the work with which one is dealing. Only then may it be possible again to build the whole thing in oneself from the kernel outward, so that every passage acquires its proper value."

We will, therefore, first try to lay bare the essential content of the introduction of the book *Theosophy*, before we can proceed to make it our own by mastering individual sentences through our own effort. In other words, we must gain a clear understanding about the real content of thought in the introduction, regardless of whether we agree with it.

Here we can proceed methodically by creating from the introduction an abstract of the bare course of the thought. To grasp the content even more precisely, we no longer need the original but can apply ourselves to our own abstract. We should find that, between the thoughts, following one another in a

---

4   *Die Modifikationen der Logik, abgeleitet aus dem Begriff des Denkens* (Leipzig: G. Brauns, 1846).

series in the abstract, even further relationships reveal themselves—that is, we can now proceed with the abstract as we did initially with the verbatim content of the introduction; we can make an abstract of the abstract and thus arrive at an even greater condensation. We can proceed in this way until we have condensed what is absolutely essential into one sentence and, finally, into a single concept. It is expected that this concept, gained through fractional distillation, will cast a brilliant light on the whole composition. We can then give an adequate and brief answer to our question: What is presented in the introduction? From this process the following results.

First Abstract (in ten sentences)

Fichte compares one who speaks of the higher things of existence with a person who has eyes but mingles with those born blind. However, since the spiritual eyes of everyone who wills it may be opened, seers of all times speak of "hidden" wisdom. Those who can experience this directly need no proof of it, but investigators of higher truth must address themselves to all human beings, who have various levels of understanding. They therefore address themselves to the feeling through which the power of truth takes hold of human beings and in which a force ultimately opens the eyes of the spirit. Erudition is not a prerequisite but a hindrance if it leads to biases. Therefore, to expand the limitations of knowledge for the ordinary human being, a process of development must be accomplished; the results of the higher research can then be grasped through sound thinking. However, to be a teacher regarding these higher realms of existence, of course, requires scientific knowledge in precisely those fields—hence, the very great responsibility of those who are spiritually commissioned. Yet, for that reason, no one should be deterred from dealing with the loftiest to which one can lift one's eyes with *Theosophy*.

Second Abstract *(in five sentences)*

Whereas ordinary human beings are blind to the spirit, there is—for all who truly want it—a possibility that the eye of the spirit may be opened. At every stage of understanding, we can approach the spiritual realms through the feeling for truth. Only those who are spiritually developed can perceive the spiritual worlds, but rational thought can grasp what the spiritual investigator communicates from those realms. No erudition is needed to perceive the spiritual, but to be a spiritual investigator requires the seer to master Spiritual Science. Through a spiritual summons, the spiritual investigator is destined to become a spiritual teacher.

Third Abstract *(in three sentences)*

The author of the book and its readers are brought face to face. The spiritual seer becomes a spiritual investigator through Spiritual Science and a spiritual teacher by being spiritually commissioned. To become a spiritual learner, the reader needs unbiased thinking, a vital feeling for truth, and goodwill.

Fourth Abstract *(in one sentence)*

The spiritual teacher, who fulfils these three prerequisites, must make three demands of the spiritual learner.

Fifth Abstract *(in one concept)*

The relationship between spiritual teacher and learner.

We can now answer our question: What is presented in the introduction? It presents the relationship between spiritual teacher and learner. At the first glance, it is not clear that this is actually the essential content. It is clear, however, that such a finding must cast a special light on every paragraph and sentence of this introduction. Readers will have to decide for themselves whether they wish to become students of the book in the sense presented in the introduction. Such a decision must be based on what the introduction has become for the reader; if it is adapted to give form to its content from the inner nature of the reader, one realizes that what seems to be the requirement of the learner by the spiritual teacher can be valid only for readers who decide, out of free will, to become students of the book. Now, however for the first time, it is valid to proceed from the total content of the introduction to penetrate its individual paragraphs and sentences. Because our decision regarding the whole book may arise right here, we must apply the maximum clarity, or judgment, to this task.

3

The Essential Nature of the Human Being

Rudolf Steiner begins his characteristic investigation of the human being.¹ He does not present theories into which we have to find our way but considers ordinary human beings with simple but sound sense, letting them, so to speak, find their own way from where they are. This is something we observe in all of Rudolf Steiner's writings; he always connects with the present and, proceeding from what we are today, he seeks the path to what is distant. Thus, we always remain connected with what we already understand and are always able to find our way back.

A quotation from Goethe leads us immediately into the nature of the human being. He shows us how we are connected with the world in a threefold way. We perceive the world about us; we receive impressions from it; and we gain knowledge about it. Rudolf Steiner describes this as follows: Human beings find the world as a given fact; they make the world a matter of personal concern to themselves; and knowledge about the world is a goal toward which human beings strive.²

---

1   See *Theosophy,* chapter 1.
2   Johann Wolfgang von Goethe (1749–1832), German poet, dramatist, novelist, and scientist. From Goethe's treatise *Der Versuch als Vermittler von Object und Subject,* "The Experiment as Mediator between Object and Subject," 1793 (Douglas Miller, ed., *Scientific Studies: Johann Wolfgang Goethe,* New York: Suhrkamp, 1988).

Rudolf Steiner introduces the image of a walk across a meadow, and from this reflection, intelligible to the very simplest thought, he draws an important item of knowledge—that the essential nature of human beings possesses three aspects. He calls these three aspects *body, soul,* and *spirit,* but warns us not to attach any preconceived meanings to these terms. Merely the fact that human beings are related to the world in a threefold way leads to the selection of definitions given.

Thus we remain entirely within the everyday world; but, meanwhile, something has already emerged within us that can lead us out of this world—knowledge that human beings are connected with the world in a threefold way. Here is a description of what Rudolf Steiner called body, soul, and spirit. The body is what we can perceive with our senses, as with any object of the outer world. On the other hand, our soul existence is our own world, inaccessible to sensory observation. Through the spirit, however, the outer world manifests to us in a different way; knowledge that the spirit brings to is independent of our emotions of soul, whether pleasure or displeasure. Steiner offers this example, "When we look up at the starry sky, the soul's experience of delight belongs to us, but the eternal laws of the stars, which we may grasp in thought and in spirit, do not belong to us. They belong to the stars" (p. 25).

"Thus as human beings we are citizens of three worlds" (ibid.). Here we see a self-evident but important conclusion. Human beings grasp the world in a threefold way—that is, the world offers us three aspects, and in this sense we must speak of three worlds: First, a world that can be perceived by means of the body; second, another world that we build for ourselves by means of our own soul; and third, a world revealed to us through our spirit.

The Bodily Nature of the Human Being

We have to observe the human body as we would minerals, plants, and animals—that is, through our bodily senses (pp. 26–28). It is clear that the human body is built up from substances of the outer world, just as the bodies of minerals, plants, and animals are. Nevertheless, these bodies are all differentiated in their structure. Our mineral body, for example, is entirely different from that of a plant, which takes in food, grows, and reproduces itself. The animal, in addition to having these functions, is capable of other activities; it makes motions and moves from place to place. Its body, therefore, must be organized differently from that of the plant to make these functions possible.

We see, then, that the forms of existence and types of activities of existence in minerals, plants, and animals are expressed in their construction, or form. Consequently, we can say, by contrast, that we can draw inferences about the form of existence represented in the mineral, the plant, and the animal on the basis of their construction.

Much importance is attached to the fact that the human body shows a characteristic difference in comparison to that of the animal, which is nearest to the human being—that is, brain structure. Thus the human body does not merely correspond to the three forms of existence—mineral, plant and animal—but also in the case of the human body, even when lying before us as a corpse, we observe something that compels us to assume a fourth form of existence, the specifically human form.

The Soul Nature of the Human Being

The characteristic of the soul is the life belonging to the soul itself (pp. 28–29). The moment anything alien or external enters the human soul entity it becomes a personal matter. This is true of even the simplest sensation. When nerves of the extremities are stimulated and conduct that stimulus to the brain, it is a simple life process. Once this stimulus is resolved into a sensation of the color red, it has become part of the inner life and belongs to the soul. This sensation leads to pleasure or displeasure, again by nature belonging to the soul, the purest inner life of the human being. Now the will is added, once more belonging to one's own life, which flows out into the world and impresses itself on the outer world.

Sensation, feeling, and will—the human soul entity functions in this threefold way. It is stimulated to action by the outer world, while the corporeality plays the role of intermediary. The body thus becomes the soul's subsoil.

The Spirit Nature of the Human Being

The first two chapters have dealt with our human relationship to the world—first, as given fact and, second, as something that concerns us personally. Now consider the goal toward which we as human beings strive: knowledge. To this end, we must point out an activity that enables us to elevate our soul life above mere dependence on sensory impressions: the activity of thinking. Through thinking we cognize things and regulate our conduct. Thus thinking, too, as well as our bodily nature, influences our soul element. The soul element exists between our bodily nature and our thinking, or spiritual nature. Human beings are subject by necessity to the laws of their bodily nature; human beings subject themselves voluntarily to the laws of thought.

Thus we can affirm that, when we are concerned with mediating the outer world with the activity of the life-permeated sense organs, we are dealing with something related to the body; but the moment what is brought within us leads to sensation, the soul element begins. Moreover, where human beings bring the laws of thinking to bear, which create knowledge of things for us and bring our life into a rational harmony, the spiritual begins. The basis for the spiritual is the psychic, for the extent to which the spirit can manifest in a human being depends on sensation and feeling, our own life.

5

Body, Soul, and Spirit

We saw in the first chapter that the construction of the human brain compels us to assume a specifically human form of existence. However, the special activity of this form of existence was not stated, but we now know what this is; it is the activity of thinking, and the brain is the physical instrument for this, just as the eye is for seeing. We have said about the body that it consists of substances of the outer world. We see now that these substances are ordered in such a way that they serve the manifestation of thought. In other words, the physical body is a mineral structure ordered in relation to the thinking spirit (see pp. 31ff).

However, this is not the whole nature of the body. What we have discovered so far is present also in a corpse, but we are investigating the nature of the living human body, which takes in nourishment, grows, and reproduces itself. Therefore, it must contain a force that invokes such phenomena—aspects that fundamentally differentiate a living body from a corpse. Such a force will be called the "life force," since it brings life to lifeless minerals. In addition, we must also call it a force that produces and maintains species, since this force calls into existence and sustains the particular character that belongs to every living creature. We see this is true by observing even the simplest plant. An acorn will, given the proper conditions, become a tree, but only an oak tree; the specific character is transmitted. Moreover, it is sustained; although the substances may change, the oak always remains an oak. The bread we eat is incorporated into our body through this force in such a way that the body does not change its essential, specific character, but is sustained. Corporeality, therefore, does not consist only of substances from the world about us, but also includes this species-forming life force.

The fact that we do not perceive this force with our senses is easily understood; we can perceive only the specific phenomena for which we possess a sensory organ; without an eye, we do not perceive light. Human beings have no sensory organ for perceiving forces. Similarly, we do not perceive electricity but only its physical manifestations (shock or light), for which we do possess organs. Imagine a person who has a sense for perceiving life forces and for whom such a force is something as real as a table or chair for us. Such a person would be able to observe this force as it acts continually in a plant and would not consider the specific nature of a plant abstractly but as having substance.

Esoteric investigators actually have such a sense. We have come to know through thinking what they have seen; in every plant, every animal, every human being esoteric investigators perceive a duplicate form filled with life; we call it the ether (or life) body. We see that the ether body transforms the structure of the physical body into an organism filled with life; in this aspect, we live the life of a plant.

However, impressions from the outer world are not merely conveyed to human beings; they become inner experience. We see that, to bring about sensation, something must be added to the ether body. The ether body mediates the life force. Plants, whose nature comprises nothing beyond the physical and ether bodies, have no sensations. The member of the human being that responds to impressions from the outer world with sensations is the sentient soul. This is not abstract to seers but real and seen. Of course, the activity of the sentient soul depends on the etheric and physical bodies, since it thrives on what they bring to it. The sentient soul's activity is therefore limited by the corporeal.

Now let us try to form an image of what Rudolf Steiner meant by the soul (or sentient) body. This will shed more light on the ether body and the sentient soul. In the ether body, a force is active that prevents the substances and materials of the physical body from following the chemical and physical laws to which they are subject by their nature as minerals. In other words, the ether body wages a continuous battle against the decay of the physical body. Through the ether body, the plant principle, which is formative, is associated with the formless, mineral principle. In the physical body, this formative principle is expressed in the cells. The maintenance of form is even exemplified in the cell, the smallest living bodily entity. The cell structure is the physical representative of the ether body.

Now we must consider the essential characteristic through which everything "animal" in nature is differentiated from the plant's nature. In contrast to the plants, which have no quality beyond the formative principle, animals possess an inner life. The inner life of animals has a soul quality, but to manifest it needs a bodily element—the soul body. The force of the soul body arranges the plant-like cells so that they become nerves and, as such, form the sense organs. Wherever nerves are present, sensation is possible. The entire physical body is woven through with nerves, so that it becomes a great apparatus of nerves and sensation. The force of the soul body thus gives us access to outer life through the sense organs. We may say that the potential of sensation is in the soul body, but that this potential can actualize only through a spiritual element behind the soul body as the recipient. This spiritual element is our spiritual being, living as the sentient soul. This actual spiritual being that we possess is usually called the *"I."* However, considered more precisely, this term is not appropriate at this stage, because only when the spiritual element lives as consciousness soul is it an "I." (We will discuss this later.) Soul body and sentient soul form a unity within the human being.

If human beings were comprised of nothing beyond the sentient soul, we could not rise above the animal (pp. 31–32). Animals follow their instincts and appetites blindly; their actions are instinctive releases that follow sensations. Human beings, however, can test and weigh sensations before acting. Through the association of thinking with sensation, the resulting actions are consciously directed toward a goal. Thinking brings clarity in regard to the outer world and helps us satisfy our impulses consciously. Rudolf Steiner shows how almost everything in modern culture serves to satisfy the needs of the sentient soul.

It is interesting to read what is said in regard to this fact in the first issue of *Luzifer*.[3] We see that the sentient soul begins to follow other laws once it is permeated by the force of thought—indeed, laws that are different by their actual nature. Thus, soul life becomes something higher. Insofar as the sentient soul is served by thinking, Rudolf Steiner calls it the rational, or intellectual, soul.

---

3   Rudolf Steiner edited the periodical *Luzifer* (later *Lucifer-Gnosis*) from 1903 to 1908. Articles discussed spiritual initiation and other subjects of Theosophy (later Anthroposophy). Those articles may be found in Rudolf Steiner, *Lucifer-Gnosis. Grundlegende Aufsätze zur Anthroposophie und Berichte aus der Zeitschrift "Luzifer" und "Lucifer-Gnosis" 1903–1908* (CW 34, Basel, 1987).

5

Manas, Budhi, and Atma

Although we have seen that human beings initially use thinking to satisfy their own needs—that is, for the purpose of raising the level of one's own life—nonetheless, this thinking leads beyond the limits of one's personal life. Consider what actually happens when we place our thinking in the service of our lower needs. We invent, for example, ships, railways, and so on; as we have seen, these are all created to serve only the lower human needs. To invent ships, railroads, and so on, we must do something else first; we must understand the laws of nature. We must know these laws before we can make them serve us; all of this means rendering the forces of nature serviceable to ourselves.

However, in coming to understand the forces of nature, people do something that leads beyond their own lives. Something similar is suggested in the example of the starry heavens (pp. 43–44). Whether, therefore, the thoughts have to do with the courses of the stars or with something else, knowledge is related not only to our own souls, but also has an independent significance. Rudolf Steiner stresses the fact that the harmony between the laws of thought and the cosmic order is a self-evident conviction to the human mind, and, moreover, that people come to know their own being through this harmony. This is obvious, since only when such harmony exists can the knowledge we gain through thinking have any value for us (pp. 44–45).

We strive to understand truths when we try to reach conclusions about the nature of phenomena. In contrast to the soul life and feelings in the soul of an individual, truths are eternal. Truth is a singular goal for everyone, no matter how varied the emotions of their souls may be. This is also true of all that is truly good; this, too, has an independent nature, unaffected by personal emotion. Therefore, when the thinking that first serves the lower needs leads us to the true and the good, it unites the soul with something eternal. All truth and goodness that the soul may bear within it is immortal.

The sentient soul, insofar as it is served by thinking, is called the "rational soul." The part of the rational soul that the true and the good (the eternal) illumine is designated the "consciousness soul." Moreover, these are not abstractions to those who possess the power of "sight." They "see" how the individual forms interpenetrate one another; how the rational soul extends beyond the sentient soul; how the consciousness soul, in turn, extends above the rational soul. What we call the "human aura" consists of these forms.

"I"-being

We may be easily tempted to consider the "I" the tenth member of the human being; at least, most people are unclear about how they should classify it (pp. 47ff). It must be stressed especially that the "I" is not separate from the other members; rather, it comprises the various members of the human being, both of soul and of spirit, insofar as they have evolved, and is one with them. This will become clearer from the following explanations.

We have considered how the "I" unites with the soul body and thus works as the sentient soul. Its activity involves this: everything brought into the soul from outside through the body as impressions is felt within us as something belonging to us. The "I," as sentient soul, responds with sensations to the stimulus communicated to it. However, it must be noted that this is true only so long as a stimulus is present; once the stimulus ceases, the sensation vanishes.

When the spiritual power of the "I" begins to give duration to the sensation—when it solidifies the sensations through its activity so that they become mental images—this spiritual power cannot express its life only as sensation; it also becomes a combining force generally called the power of thought. This activity of the spiritual power of the "I" is essentially different from what is expressed in sensation. Where mental images arise (thus where memory exists), there is also the possibility of evoking spiritual content again for oneself. In sensations, the spiritual power of the "I" remains passive; it is the recipient of the stimuli brought to it. However, as combining power it draws from its own depths; it becomes active—indeed, creatively active.

Consequently, this activity is attributed to a special region of the soul. The part of the soul that merely receives sensations we call the sentient soul; the thinking soul we call the rational soul. The results of this combining power of the "I" are given to us in technological achievements such as railroads, telegraph, and so on. This combining power, however, works only as a preparation for the fact that it ("I"-being, which has become abstract in thought) knows how to differentiate its own activity from everything else. It directs itself toward things and thus achieves awareness of those things; it directs itself toward itself, toward its own activity, and thus attains to self-awareness. Only through this last activity is "I"-consciousness fully achieved. We see now that everything we have thus far called the spiritual power of the "I" did not yet deserve this designation; the term *"I"* refers to this power only at this stage. When the power of the soul thus becomes aware of its own spiritual being, or "I"-being, the eternal begins to shine within the soul. Everything within the soul that has the character of the eternal is comprehended as the "consciousness soul."

We see that the "I" attains consciousness of itself—that is, it recognizes itself as spirit from spirit. The "I" thus grows beyond what was hitherto its standard of measure, rising above the sphere of "its own." In the consciousness soul the standard of "its own" measure remains, but the "I" now overcomes itself; it no longer takes its measure from itself, but from what it cognizes. Therefore we read in *Theosophy:* "...but the 'I' gives itself over to the spirit in order to be filled by it" (p. 50). The "I" pours itself out over the spiritual world, which it knows. Through this surrender to the spiritual world, it attains the beginning of intuition. Just as the manifestation of the physical is called *sensation,* likewise Rudolf Steiner called the revelation of the spiritual *intuition.* Moreover, everything that penetrates from the spiritual world into the human being must manifest through the "I." Something occurs here that is similar to the change by which the corporeal, through the soul body, becomes a bodily organ of perception. Here the "I," which previously lived as the soul, becomes an organ through which the spiritual world opens itself. The "I" living thus as organ of intuition, knowing itself as spirit, is called *spirit self.*

Much can be added to what Rudolf Steiner has said about *budhi* and *atma.* For these sublime members of the human being, attained only in the remote future, cannot be made more accessible to our understanding without the danger of evoking materialistic images.

We may say the physical body exists as a primordial form in the thought of the Godhead and is manifest in the spiritual world as *atma*, or *spirit body*.[1] Only those who participate at the level of the Godhead can make statements about it. *Budhi*, or *life spirit*, is the name given to the medium through which this spiritual primordial form becomes a living being. Budhi, the spiritual life force, works in the "I" as an unconscious, but goal-seeking, force that elevates the "I" from unconsciousness to self-aware. When this force within a human being becomes aware of its eternal and divine nature, it becomes the means for bringing the primordial form of the spirit body (*atma*) to spiritual manifestation.

---

[1] Rudolf Steiner here uses the term *Geistesmensch* (lit. "spirit human being"). In theosophical language and in the earliest editions of *Theosophy* itself, it is called *atman* (as spirit self is called *manas* and life spirit *budhi*). It is clear from this context (pp. 53ff) and from the conclusion—that the Geistesmensch, or "spirit human being," is the physical body transformed by the "I"—that "spirit body" (atma) is actually the most unambiguous and least confusing translation of that term (fn. *Theosophy*, p. 54).

6

Re-embodiment of the Spirit and Destiny

The soul is the intermediary between body and spirit, between the present moment and eternity. It condenses into concepts the fleeting sensations of the body, and gives permanence to these concepts through memory, thus approaching the spiritually eternal. Through action, it imprints eternity upon the transitory. Every action attains permanence, since it changes the surrounding world and thus causes effects that in turn become the causes of future effects (pp. 64ff).

Through manifest physicality, the soul receives impressions from the surrounding world. The soul preserves those impressions and later unites with new experiences; thus, remembering comes into existence. Through remembering, the soul imparts what it has received through the body to the spirit. The eternal laws of goodness and truth, as well as the memories brought to it through the soul, live in the human spirit. However, memories do not remain in the spirit in their original form; the spirit draws from them the force needed to raise the level of their capacities. The experiences of the body become memories of the soul, and these become capacities of the spirit (p. 66).

We can explain the human body on the basis of the laws of heredity; it recapitulates the form of its progenitors. We can explain the human spirit on the basis of the laws of reincarnation; it is a recapitulation of itself. This is clear from biography when we consider it correctly. The soul, as intermediary between body and spirit, participates in each—in the body, since it permeates the soul body as sentient soul, and in the spirit, because, as the consciousness soul, it interpenetrates the spirit self. The sentient soul transforms the soul body according to the nature of the soul, but the sentient body is inherited, and it thus inherits the personal characteristics of the progenitors, whereby the physical heredity receives its soul element.

In our life, the spirit self blends with the consciousness soul. Thus it mediates the laws of the true and the good to the soul. The experiences of the soul are, in turn, mediated through the consciousness soul to the spirit—they come to expression in the spirit self as capacities. The reincarnating spirit self brings the capacities it has gained in previous lives with it.

What we do one day becomes our destiny for the next day. Thus our actions in one life become our destiny for the next life. The surrounding world has been modified by human actions. Thus a connection, or interrelationship, exists between the spirit and the effects of the action, since the capacities of the spirit and the acts in the surrounding world have come from the same source—the soul's experiences. The reincarnating spirit therefore finds a sourrounding world that corresponds to the actions of the preceding life.

The body is subject to the law of heredity. The soul is subject to self-created destiny (karma). The spirit is subject to the law of reincarnation. From this we can draw the following analysis:

Analysis

A. Introduction: The soul is mediator between body and spirit through (1) memory and (2) action

B. Exposition

1. The soul retains the experiences in memory.	1. The spirit imparts impulses of will to the soul.
2. The spirit draws its capacities from the soul's experiences	2. The soul flows through action into the surrounding world.

Intermediate Reflection: The presupposition for considering the soul's mediation beyond birth and death:

Heredity and Reincarnation

1. The soul, by union of sentient soul and sentient body, give something to heredity.	1. The spirit comes into relationship with a soul whose destiny is fixed by the actions of the previous life.
2. The spirit, through the union of spirit self and consciousness soul, bring the fruits of the previous life.	2. In a physical sense, the place of incarnation is fixed through action.

DIAGRAM OF THE PRECEDING ANALYSIS

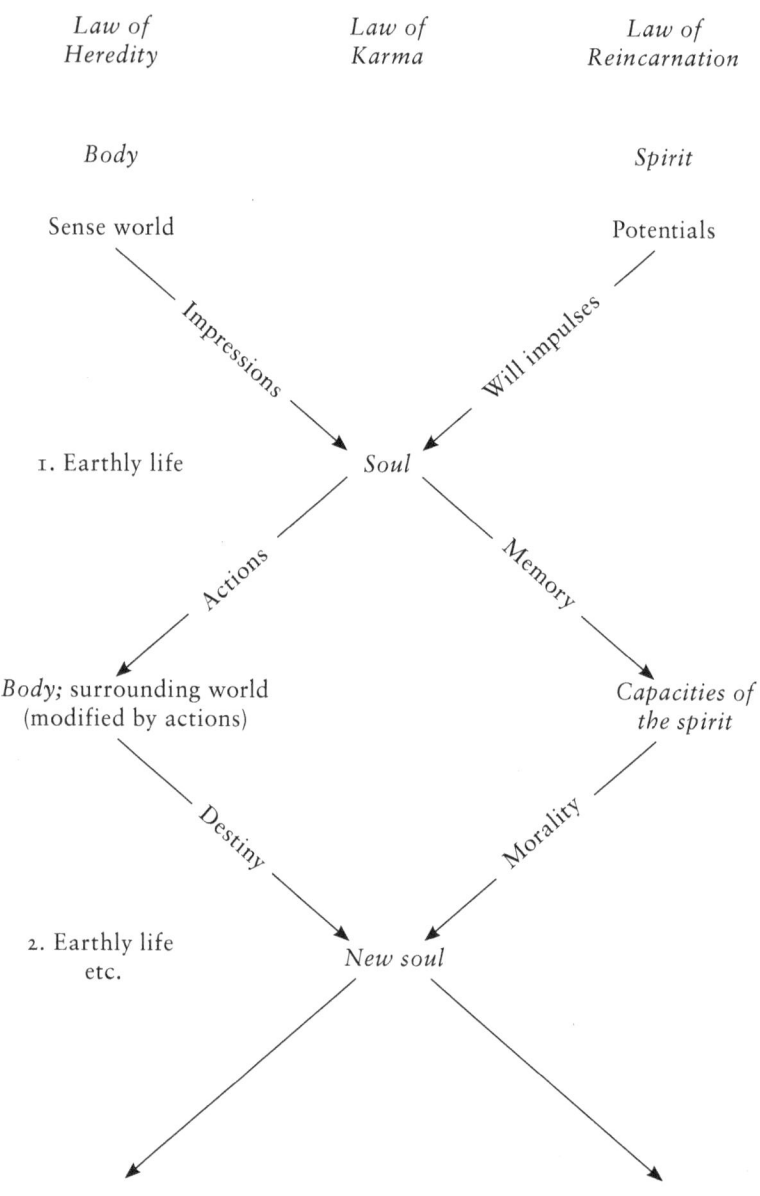

Explanation of the Diagram

The impressions of the body are brought, through the soul's memory, to the spirit as capacities.

The spirit gives impulses of will to the soul; through action the soul flows into the surrounding world.

In both cases the soul mediates. Thus a relationship arises between 1) the surrounding world modified by the soul's actions and 2) the spirit in Devachan enriched by the soul.[1]

The spirit is led back to the earth through this relationship and a new soul formed. This soul experiences new impressions from a surrounding world modified by actions, and these impressions represent destiny coming from the previous incarnation.

On the other hand, the spirit enters its incarnation with the potentials that manifested through impressions conveyed by the soul in the previous life. New impulses of will flow from these potentials. Thus human life advances through reincarnation.

Commentary and Explanation Based on this Chapter

It is most important here to recall the definitions already given for body, soul, and spirit. An understanding of this chapter is closely connected with these, since the whole development of reincarnation and Karma comes about by closely following these definitions.

Body allows the external world to come into relationship with human beings.

---

[1] *Devachan,* a compound word from Sanskrit: *deva* = gods, and the Tibetan *chan* = land, indicating the "dwelling of the gods" according to the theosophical teachings of H. P. Blavatsky. Devachan is considered the place where most souls go after death, where desires are gratified, corresponding to the Christian Heaven. However, Devachan is a temporary, intermediate state of being before the soul's eventual rebirth back into the physical world.

Soul allows human beings to create a life of their own.

Spirit manifests to human beings when they permit things to speak about themselves.

We need also to distinguish adequately between sentient soul and rational soul. Perception presupposes a physical body permeated by an astral body. Thus the potential for sensation arises. Before this possibility can become an actuality, a spiritual being, as recipient, must exist behind all this. This is the "I," which appears here as sentient soul.

The mental image consisting in a condensed sensation must be clearly differentiated from sensation. This is brought about in turn through the spiritual force of the "I," which nonetheless lives through the force of the ether body as rational soul.

7

Perceiving in the Soul World

Thinking is a faculty through which the truly essential—the real, with real being—manifests in nature. All science consists of presenting what has being, the real; it adds thinking to mere observation. Science is thus compelled by thinking to distinguish among the qualities of mineral, plant, and animal.[1] Therefore, we have the differences in actual being among these three kingdoms of nature determined by their forms of manifestation.

There is another science that likewise includes human beings as objects of study, but it considers human beings not merely as a living creatures, as zoology does, but as spiritually active beings. This science is history; it considers the essential activating principle to be the biographies of historic personalities. Just as "species" is the essential element in biology, "biography" is the essence of history. What pertains to the species in the animal corresponds to biography in human beings (see chapter 3).

---

1   The animal kingdom, from the perspective of zoology, consists of the various species. All that is important in the animal consists of the species' unique characteristics. In zoology, humankind figures as the highest creature of the animal kingdom.

The Three Worlds

The three worlds are not presented in such a way that they must be simply accepted as the results of observation and reported to us by a clairvoyant. Rather—and this is the essential point—the three worlds are discovered by observing the human being. We have seen, for example, that the physical body can be investigated through the senses, but that this method fails when we apply it to the soul. We need a different means of observation to investigate the soul and yet another for the spiritual; in this case, not only does the physical mode of observation fail, but also the soul, which measures through what belongs to ourselves. In addition, it becomes clear that these three members of the human being correspond to three worlds (pp. 93ff). Our threefold existence can be discovered by all human beings within themselves; we can live in thought through this same investigation, which has great importance.

The standard by which we can measure anything said about the soul world is, as we know, what belongs to us. However, we cannot gain any experience or research content by simply remaining within the soul.

To understand this, we must consider what we need to comprehend an object in the physical world. We need to stand face to face with these things when we consider the phenomena of the physical world. We must not be within them. Only in contrast to the non-"I" can the "I" develop. The "I" must confront the non-"I"; only then can it become conscious of that non-"I" and distinguish itself from it. Previously, everything was undifferentiated. Something similar occurs in the soul world. On the astral plane, we have no objective consciousness; things present themselves to us there—not outwardly, but only within. However, to observe and to investigate them we need the capacity to separate ourselves from them. We must feel that we are just as separate from them as we are from objects in the physical world. We must gain an objective consciousness ("I"-consciousness) in the astral world to gain our own direct knowledge. For this we must have soul organs of perception, analogous to our sensory organs in the physical world. Through such perceptual organs, the soul world existing outside our own being comes into contact with us and can be investigated (pp. 96ff).

How should we understand this process of approaching, with objective consciousness, a world whose very characteristic is that it is our own? We must simply withdraw our "I"-being from what is our own. What is part of us must become an organ—the cognizing "I"—through which we measure "our own"; it must face our own "I" objectively. We must not be inwardly united with what we are, but first separate ourselves from them and then, through our will, reunite with them (pp 103ff). This is more difficult than generally believed; when people claim to face their own soul nature objectively, this is rarely true. What actually occurs is a later reflection in thought; at the moment of the feeling, such objectivity is not present. With our own soul being, we need to stand face to face with our sensation, our own experience, at the very moment of that experience, as though a separate observer. This requires the soul to stand as something solid before the impressions. A comparison from the physical world will make this clear.

If our physical body were fluid—that is, with every thrust from without it could assume the form of what gives the thrust and could harmonize immediately with the form of everything acting upon it externally—we would never experience the sensation of touch. It is only through resistance that the physical body opposes impressions from without and mediates to us the sense of touch. It is like this also in the psychic world. The soul assumes the form, as it were, of every impression that acts upon it; every impression takes it captive, and it offers no resistance. However, if the soul is to meet the soul world as a sensory organ, it must become "solid" and capable of offering resistance.

We see that the soul sense organs presuppose a boundary that is essentially different from the boundary between our astral body and the soul world. Of course, we cannot deal here with substantial concepts; rather, it is feelings that are separated. In the world of instincts and feelings, a body of feelings is created. In ordinary life it is not we ourselves who create our feelings; they are stimulated in us from without. We must now learn to become free of those stimulations and to create our feelings through our own forces. How this comes to pass is set forth in chapter 4, "The Path to Knowledge." This sum total of the feelings we ourselves create then forms that boundary and exerts resistance, which is needed to generate an objective perception—objective consciousness, or "I"-consciousness—on the astral plane.

Thus our perceptual organs are made up of what constitutes the soul world—that is, the world of feelings.

8

Sensory Observation, Thinking, and Cognition

In all that we have considered thus far, we have found that only thought creates the truly real. When we first realize this, every sense experience seems unreal to us. However, this arises only from the fact that we have not yet followed the theory of knowledge through to its conclusion. In fact, we discover through thought the real, toward which all cognition pursues its course only when thought is associated with sensory observation.

Knowledge of reality is comprised of sensory observation plus thinking. The fact that reality flows to it from two sides is caused by our organization. To understand this, we must simply investigate in thought our sensory observation in its own nature. We then learn to differentiate the essential from the fortuitous. We do not remain with the "how" but press forward to the actually effectual element of sensory observation. In other words, we then find in all sensory observation that something is involved that is accessible to us in thought. We find, for example, that what is essential in the sensation and the actual "what" is a concept. In what presents itself to us in sensation as a certain form or color, the concept "tree," for example, which is directly accessible to our thought, manifests itself. We see from this that sensory observation without thought can give us nothing more than a chaotic complex, but that thinking without sensory observation cannot bring an object before us; only the two together give us the reality "tree." The tree as such, however, is a unity. The fact that we grasp it in two parts is because of our own organization. Thus the whole world is also a unity; we tear it apart because of our organization, and we reunite it into a unity through the act of cognition.

Perception plays the same role in the astral realm, where it is necessary to unite the right concepts with observations to attain knowledge. Esoteric investigators, therefore, never merely impart to us their observations but bring them to us in the form of thoughts and precepts. If they designated what they had observed as "something with brown spots," for example, this would mean nothing to us. Only when the concept is united with this—when they explain that one or another passion manifests itself in this color—does it become an object of knowledge for us.

PART TWO

Principles of Spiritual Science

1

The "I" and the Nature of the Human Being

There is a method of presenting the theories of Spiritual Science, or Anthroposophy, that, in a certain sense, involves a complete reversal of all we are used to hearing. *Epistemology* is the term we will give this method of exposition, because it forces students of this wisdom back onto their own principles of knowledge. By contrast, such a method of exposition can also be to show how a self-consistent theory of knowledge, as commonly practiced today, offers little to the needs of philosophy. Yet it can be highly fruitful and positive for human knowledge and is by no means forced to stay within the fetters riveted to it in the present stage of spiritual life. Moreover, this kind of epistemology does not need to restrict itself to presenting the forms of cognition but holds a distinctive and essential content of its own, which shows how near philosophical reflection comes to the teachings of Spiritual Science if only it remains true to itself.

It is only natural that the way of presenting doctrines as given by spiritual investigators would also be retained by those who make those doctrines the subject of their own research or whose task it is to propagate them. But it is precisely when we feel the need to adapt, to the best of our ability, the teachings entrusted to us to life that we have to be struck by the fact that the message of a spiritual investigator is garbed in a specific form and that those experiences in higher worlds are not communicated as they were experienced. Rather, a spiritual investigator must sharply distinguish between descriptions of experiences in the higher worlds and what is communicated as truth, or doctrine, about the world and human beings. This specific form addresses understanding; it connects what we already know or ought to know.

Spiritual investigators use our own cognitive forms of thought as the garb for their experiences. This presupposes, however, that we should know and command our own forms of cognition, and that we should also be convinced of their suitability to apprehend reality. This presupposition is not in our consciousness when we deal with the less complex areas of Spiritual Science and are still able to connect with familiar experiences. However, as the results communicated to us by the spiritual investigator advance into the higher realms of being, the greater, too, is our lack of epistemological inner certainty. We feel an increasingly insistent call and admonition when, in those loftier expositions, a spiritual investigator begins to connect with the finer threads of the cognitive faculty for our understanding. We cannot follow the spiritual investigator with our own understanding into the heights of spiritual investigation unless we have realized the certain presence of the spirit in ourselves. Therefore, our first goal must be to understand the reality of spirit.

We call our own spiritual nature "I," and it is immediately clear to our minds that all knowledge and search for reality is most intimately connected with our "I"-being. In Spiritual Science, we come to know the "I" as the fourth member of the human being. We are taught that human beings consist of the physical body, which contains all mineral properties; the etheric body, which carries the plant properties such as growth, nutrition, procreation; the astral body, which carries the animal properties of instincts, desires, passions, and so on; and of the "I," which raises human beings above the beasts and assigns us to our own human kingdom. When we come to know the "I" in this way, we run the risk of contemplating it from without, so to speak, regarding it perhaps like the other, lower members of the human nature as a kind of "body." In doing so, we position ourselves as separate from our "I," as if it were another thing in the outside world. However, nothing could be more incorrect.

Above all, spiritual investigators are deeply concerned with showing that the "I" is the core of the human being, which cannot, for that very reason, be described in external terms but must be apprehended inwardly by each individual. This is brought home to us when we are made aware that the word *"I"* indicates a name that, when it reaches our ear from outside, can never refer to oneself. Anyone can call a table a "table," but we can say "I" only about ourselves as individuals. Yet we are open to the danger described, which never allows us to apprehend fully what is spiritual. This is because, when the other members are being described to us, we are already presumed to have inwardly apprehended our "I," since an appeal is made to our powers of knowledge that, in fact, achieve their development through the "I" uniting with the object of cognition. This can be stated as a general truth. When we are therefore guided by the spiritual investigator through the members of the human being's essential nature, up to the "I," it may dawn upon us that we need to contemplate the "I" first, apprehending our "I" itself, which is presupposed on our journey. This, then, can only lead to epistemological reflections that must begin with this very "I." Thus arises a seeming reversal, which was mentioned at the beginning. The spiritual investigator connects with what we already know and leads us to the "I." Our knowledge, however, is connected precisely with that "I" and must start from it.

It cannot be the task now to furnish a detailed theory of knowledge but merely propose to mention a few main principles. All cognition proceeds between the "I" and what we may comprehensively term *not-"I."* The "I" seeks the reality of the not-"I" and doing so presupposes its own reality. This, however, is feasible only if the "I" is capable of apprehending its own reality. This is the main task confronting the theory of knowledge. Hence, we can also formulate the task of the theory of knowledge with a question: What is reality? In so doing we must keep in mind that the "I" can find reality and, with it, the foundation of all knowledge only in itself.

If we would really attempt to apprehend the "I" in its abstract purity, we must ask ourselves precisely how the "I" as such is distinguished from the not-"I." First, it is only by the same means that other objects are also distinguished from one another—by judgment, or thought. Thought, of course, is not the only so-called content of the "I." Nevertheless, the "I" itself becomes conscious of all that can fill it as sensations, feelings, impulses of the will, and the like only through the mental images and concepts connected with them—that is, through thought. Through all that fills the "I," thought is linked with the not-"I," from which it has received its stimulus. The "I" establishes a relationship with itself only through the mental images and concepts connected with it. Thought first makes the "I" to be the "I." All other properties establish relationships between "I" and not-"I"; thought establishes the relationship of the "I" to itself. Hence, we can apprehend the "I," the prime reflective, when we let the force—by virtue of which the "I" is distinguished from all else—turn back upon itself. In other words, we must envision thought as it is *after* all that we call not-"I" has been made abstract. Thought about thought; this is the formula stating that the "I" is concerned only with its own essence.

Thought about thought ("observation of thinking"[1]) is the point upon which the epistemological section of Rudolf Steiner's *Philosophy of Spiritual Activity* hinges and echoes other thoughts expressed here. In that book, the unique significance of this formula for knowledge is indicated for the first time, and our own reflections follow different paths, despite their inner kinship, and show us how impossible it is to answer epistemological questions without that formula as a foundation.

Now what is left if thought concerns itself only with thought—that is, if the "I" disregards everything that protrudes from the not-"I" into the "I"? There is nothing save the forms of thought, all the laws, and the properties we enunciate in logic. In a comprehensive sense, we may call this the world of pure thought. When the "I" lives in pure thought, it is alone with its innermost being. Indeed, we can designate what lives in thought about thought the pure "I." In observation of thinking we have the sum of the purest essence of the "I." However, the formula "thinking about thinking"—or, more accurately, observation of thinking—contains something else of utmost significance. In anything else that can fill consciousness, we must distinguish between the content itself and the

---

[1] "Observation of thinking" is discussed in greater detail in *Intuitive Thinking as a Spiritual Path: A Philosophy of Freedom*, chapter 3, "Thinking in the Service of Understanding the World," especially pp. 31ff.

form in which that content presents itself. In the observation of thinking, we apprehend the only point where both coincide. The thought that forms the content is the same as the thought applied to it. The forms take a course precisely according to the rules that make up the content. That, however, is exactly what we were seeking.

Here we have content upheld by its own form, or a form that has its own essence for content. Here we surely have something that exists through itself, independent of everything else! Thus we have developed a concept that we can designate by a name usually applied to every kind of thing, except the one for which it is most suited—that is, reality. We call reality only what exists through itself and nothing else. Reality must emerge when thought is focused upon itself.

Now we must ask: What emerges as reality in pure thought? Observation of thinking yields the laws of logic first. They, of course, are not reality as such. Reality must be something in which all that is highest and purest in pure thought is gathered into one point, comprising in itself everything that can be called pure thought. It is true that in all discussions of logic thought moves in its own domain, but at any given time it does so only with a part of itself, as it were. In the end, this is what the reality of observation of thinking must be.

In fact, we can find such a point when we begin to make a simple analysis of thought. In doing so we can adhere to the course of logical theory as universally presented, but we must always focus on the essential. Logic begins with the classification of concepts and moves on to combine the concepts into judgments, and then to unite the judgments into conclusions. Now a simple act of reflection shows us that all thought proceeds entirely by the means of concepts. Since conclusions are made up of judgments, it is enough to show that judgments are made up wholly of concepts.

Let us just take a simple judgment: Human beings are mortal. Here we have first the subjective concept "human beings" and the predicative concept "mortal." Both are linked by the so-called linking verb are. That little word expresses the fact that, of two concepts, one can be a subjective and the other a predicative concept. Now, if we look closely at the matter, we see that this, too, is a definite concept, which we might designate with the word *predictability*. It is a concept expressed in all judgments. Thus, all combinations of concepts, or even judgments, are again definite concepts. In this way we have narrowed observation of thinking so that we now need to deal with concepts alone. However, the individual concepts are different; their differentiation is indeed precisely what we are taught in the conceptual theory of logic.

The important thing for us is that the concepts have varying degrees of purity. Thus, for example, the predicative concept is always purer than the subjective concept in a judgment, since it is precisely the meaning of judgment that the relatively less pure subjective concept will be clarified in the purity of the predicative concept. Nonetheless, our task is to find the point in pure thought that draws all particulars together. However, this must be a concept, since thought proceeds only by way of concepts. It must be the highest and purest concept, comprising in itself all that is conceptual. We can express such a concept, and it represents the highest elaboration of thought, the highest abstraction, but at the same time comprises in itself all pure thought. It is the concept of the concept.

Now, what does this formula express? We must be clear in our minds that the concept as form always comprehends what may vary as content. Thus, the concept "chair" comprehends all the possible forms that a chair may assume. It follows that, similarly, the concept of a concept must, as a form, comprehend all the variations that conceptual content may assume. It is, therefore, the sum and substance of all potential thoughts of the thinking faculty. Nonetheless, there remains a difference between the formula—concept of the concept—and the thinking faculty, as we will see even more clearly later. Whereas the faculty is something like a form, which may also remain empty, the concept of the concept presupposes the use of that faculty until, in its highest development, it has its innermost essence for content. It is like the starting point and the end point of a circle; they actually coincide. In any case, in that highest abstraction we have precisely what we get when we strip the "I" of all that derives from the not-"I." *Hence, the concept of the concept is the pure "I."* We see immediately that we have concentrated in the formula "concept of the concept" all that we could say about "observation of thinking." Here, too, we have a form that has its own essence for content, a content that is carried by its own form.

The concept of the concept, or pure "I," is the reality that emerges in the course of observation of thinking. The pure "I" is reality. It is remarkable that we have found reality in the highest abstraction, but by our path we have also accomplished the Rosicrucian tenet, which, as the starting point of the Rosicrucian ascent to higher stages of being, has once more been made accessible to us by Spiritual Science. It states, *"In pure thought you find the 'I,' which can maintain itself."*

We have found a fixed point, a beginning of understanding, and a reality, as well as the standard for all that we are seeking as understanding of reality. Reality is what exists through itself and nothing else. This standard is taken from the reality of the "I"-being, which apprehends itself, and with this we can now address ourselves to what approaches us from the not-"I"—to what we may call observation in every form. First, however, we still have to elaborate a few concepts that will show us how close we have come to certain fundamental principles of Spiritual Science. We should not avoid such elaborations, much the way we might generally avoid empty conceptual molds; here we connect to a primal concept that is a vital reality that we must positively designate as a being, the pure "I."

We said at the beginning that all cognition advances as between "I" and not-"I." The "I" seeks the reality of the not-"I" by assuming its own reality. We have found that the "I" can indeed apprehend its own reality, therefore it seems wholly permissible to attempt such a path to knowledge whereby the "I" extends its own standard of reality to the not-"I." In fact, all of the knowledge that is accessible to us—including all scientific knowledge—follows this path, although we can still give a far deeper justification to it than is usual, as we shall see. Nevertheless, we must certainly not assume that it is the only path to knowledge. If knowledge is to establish a relation between two factors, "I" and not-"I," then it can be only one of several possibilities if the factor assumes a preferential position in relation to the other because the standard for the other is taken from it.

In all thought constructs, it is most important to maintain complete harmony among all the notes sounded. Avoidance of any partiality is the first prerequisite if reflections in thought are to lead to a complete result. Thus, we must at least envision the possibility that there may be a cognition in which the other factor plays a predominant part in its turn, whereby reality is not determined according to the standard of the "I," but according to the standard of the not-"I." Moreover, we must even allow the possibility of a third kind of knowledge, in which neither of the factors predominates, so that knowledge arises through mutual penetration. For us both cases are no more than a possibility of thought, but only until we find ourselves faced with the results of knowledge thus constituted. We may then be led positively to acknowledge such results if we have previously discovered the possibility of such knowledge in thought.

Now such results may actually be found. This is the nature of Spiritual Science in particular; its knowledge and ordinary knowledge are gained in different ways. We are shown how all human relationships assume a different form as we rise to higher stages of existence, where things no longer confront us as sharply separated; thus with them we feel, by contrast, as being apart. The "I" extends its domain to include things; it feels united with them in a kind of inward equilibrium. Things begin to reveal their inwardness to those who are clairvoyant, so that they can feel with them as with beings of their own kind. This description of the stage of knowledge that Spiritual Science provides agrees fully with the case we found possible, whereby "I" and not-"I" are in equilibrium. That stage is known as *imagination knowledge*.

The third stage is described to us by spiritual investigators—that human beings begin to creep into things, so to speak; we no longer stand in contrast to them, but experience them within our inner being. Thus a complete reversal takes place in the relationship we know between "I" and not-"I." It is the stage Spiritual Science calls *inspiration knowledge,* a stage at which the "I" no longer applies its standard of reality to the not-"I," but finds its own reality, a new and higher reality, in the not-"I."

Within the whole broad area of what encircles human beings, initiates at this stage find their "I"—the *higher self* as described in inspired writings. It is a false view to look for the higher self in our own inner being; there we are left alone with ourselves. At best, we find the pure "I" and can no longer get away from ourselves. We may even lose ourselves in egoism unless we turn to the not-"I." The higher self lies outside, and there we must find it. This is what we are told by spiritual investigators.

Thus, we have found three stages of knowledge:

1. The "I" predominates: intellectual knowledge.
2. "I" and not-"I" in equilibrium: imagination knowledge.
3. The not-"I" predominates: inspiration knowledge.

Spiritual Science speaks of these three worlds. We also see from our exposition that these three worlds are not separate from but exist within one another. The world that reveals itself depends on the stage of development of the one who contemplates. We see further that to ascend to higher worlds requires us to step completely out of ourselves; this can be achieved only by the methods shown by Spiritual Science. In this way we cannot understand the immediate apperceptions of spiritual investigators, but only after they have clothed knowledge in the forms of our understanding—that is, when it is communicated in the form of thoughts and doctrines, as stated at the beginning of our reflections. Such "stepping out of oneself" should be distinguished, of course, from what we do when we approach the not-"I" with our standard of reality derived from the "I," so that we do not remain fixed in the "I," or egoism, in which case separation would, of course, actually persist. We certainly can understand, however, how this more theoretical passing beyond one's self may be the first requirement for ascending to higher worlds, and it is, above all, part of this that the "I" will first have truly apprehended itself.

This points us back again to the part of our enquiry where we saw how the "I" first detaches itself from the not-"I." Just as we see a confluence of the "I" with the not-"I" toward the future in the ascent of the human being, so, too, the separation of the "I" must be preceded by a state in the past in which "I" and not-"I" formed a unity. Also in this direction we can, in a strictly analogous way, distinguish three stages in the relationship between the two. The first stage is where the "I" can focus itself, where it is, in a state of separation. The second, preceding the latter, is one where the relationships tend from the "I" to the not-"I" and, vice versa, where a sort of equilibrium is maintained. The third stage, even further removed, is where the "I" itself does not yet exist at all, but only its possibility is present in the not-"I."

Now, without further ado, we can call the stage at which the "I" can apprehend itself the spiritual stage, where the human spirit breaks out into the open. The stage at which the relationships exist reciprocally—at which the "I" acts on the not-"I" and the not-"I" on the "I"—points to the human soul. The third stage, at which the "I" is present only as potential in the not-"I," as it were, is the expression for the human body. We are even in a position to give a conceptual expression to the finer transitions, and here again our results tally with those obtained by the spiritual investigator. In this enquiry, too, we must begin from above—that is, at the point from which our concepts derive. There we may call the pure "I," born in pure thought, the first point of our true spirituality. This is the germ of what Spiritual Science called *spirit self,* while the higher stages of knowledge are connected with the development of the members Spiritual Science calls *life spirit* and *spirit body*.

Observation of thought, or life in the realm of pure thought, is the precondition for the emergence of pure "I," the spiritual spark. We may equate that sphere with what Spiritual Science calls the consciousness soul, or spiritual soul. It provides the transition from the spiritual in human beings, where our "I" has apprehended itself, to the soul, where it is still bound up with the not-"I." This latter state may also be described as the precondition of the consciousness soul, in that we must have the capacity to think before that thought can focus on itself as object. We thereby obtain an expression for the *intellectual* (or mind) *soul;* it denotes the state in which the "I" draws its content from the not-"I." Also, for this, it once again needs a foundation, or state, in which the not-"I" can now penetrate to the "I," to which the term *"I"* does not yet, at this stage, properly apply in order to give it its stimuli. This is denoted by the expression *sentient soul*. With this, we enter the sphere of the not-"I," insofar as it bears within itself the precondition for an "I"—that is, into the sphere of corporeality, which Spiritual Science calls *sentient body*.

Thus, to the degree that the sphere of the "I" extends, human nature presents itself to us as the direct result of the theory of knowledge. This is, of course, no accident but in fact a guarantee that our theory of knowledge, as previously outlined, attains the mark. It is consonant with the very nature of a theory of knowledge that it should give us information about human beings in relation to the world—that is, above all, about our own nature.

From this, it seems that we are also justified in rejecting a theory of knowledge and its objections if it does not lead to a positive result or real content. Nevertheless, the purpose of an epistemology, or theory of knowledge, will certainly not be fulfilled by formal epistemological statements that force us to conclude that human beings can have absolutely no "objective" knowledge of the world, that we cannot transcend our own views, that all knowledge must be "subjective," and so on. Such a result is completely self-destructive. Such an assumption amounts to sawing off the branch on which we are sitting; it is this very knowledge—about which it is asserted that it cannot lead to reality—that is used and presumed valid for us to make that assertion. If all knowledge is subjective—that is, according to the usual meaning of this word, unreal—then, too, "knowing" that human beings cannot have objective knowledge is surely equally subjective or unreal.

Such self-contradiction, however, is very much the nature of today's thinking, as Rudolf Steiner has shown in *The Philosophy of Spiritual Activity*. All such results clearly bear the stamp of their origin in materialistic thinking; it is typical of materialistic "truths" that they cancel themselves. Thus, a saying that is so often used—especially as an argument against the adherents of Spiritual Science—is "No brain, no thought." This saying is intended to express the truth that all thoughts are products of the brain—in other words, subjective productions of the organism, from which it follows that thinking is naturally subjective and can determine nothing about objective reality. Where materialism is less sharply defined, such a statement at least means that thoughts are connected to the physical brain; therefore our inquiry must start with the brain. In any case, this very idea is used and its accuracy presumed to support the statement "No brain, no thought." This and similar arguments must not, therefore, be allowed to disturb us in our inquiries; rather, we must maintain the position that thought can apprehend only itself. Spirit can be grasped only by raising oneself to it, not by drawing it down to us.

We defined the sphere of the "I" and through pure reasoning reached the not-"I" from two directions. From one direction the path led up to sensory perception; from the other it led to suprasensory intuition. It behooves us now to address ourselves to the not-"I" to become acquainted with the value and epistemological significance of contemplation or perception, since the "I" can acquire content for cognition only by going beyond itself to the not-"I," beginning with what comes to it from the not-"I." That is generally the object of observation. If the "I" stays within itself then clearly it can know only its own reality and may lose itself in egoism to the degree that it doubts everything else (*Solipsism*[2]). In our conceptual enquiries we are led right up to the boundary of the "I," which is also the boundary of the not-"I." From that point on, we may not simply go forward as from the "I" but must look for the not-"I," such as it is for the not-"I."

We must now recall that the "I" can apprehend itself only by first detaching itself from the not-"I"; everything had to be excluded from thought that derives from the not-"I." The two concepts "I" and not-"I" came into being simultaneously; they condition each other. Thus, the same rights must accrue to the not-"I" as to the "I" from the moment the latter comes into being; both must bear a kind of relationship. This is not implicit,

---

[2] Solipsism (from Latin *solus,* meaning "alone," and *ipse,* meaning "self") is the philosophical idea that only one's own mind is sure to exist. As an epistemological position, solipsism holds that knowledge of anything outside one's own mind is uncertain. Accordingly, we cannot know the outer world and other minds, and therefore they might not exist beyond one's own mind. As a metaphysical position, solipsism goes further to conclude that the world and other minds do not exist.

of course, in the pure conceptual negation in the term *not-"I,"* since horse and non-horse, for instance, do not in any way need to be related to each other. It shows itself in this, however, that the separation of "I" from the not-"I" is an actual, thoroughly real process, as already shown.

This becomes even clearer when we recall that a true transition takes place from the "I" to the not-"I," up to the point where we found the possibility of the "I" in the not-"I" (corporeity). Thus, it is really the not-"I" that continues itself up to the point where it becomes an "I," so that the "I" presents itself as a part of the not-"I," if one may say which part detaches itself by directing itself upon itself. The "I" itself withdraws from the not-"I" and opposes itself to it as "I." Now the "I" is to unite again with the not-"I," and this can come about through the "I" giving back, as it were, to the not-"I" what it had taken from it; this is, primarily, *pure thought*.

Now the next question is this: Where can the "I" begin to work with pure thought? Where can it find the not-"I"? Evidently, at the very place where the "I" began to detach itself and that, in the sense of Spiritual Science, we designated the sentient soul and sentient body. Here, we must not overlook a twofold possibility. One was mentioned previously—the possibility of an "I" forming itself in the not-"I." The other is that now the "I" will find the not-"I" again. This meeting of "I" and not-"I" is expressed by the term *sensory perception*. According to Spiritual Science, this occurs through the cooperation of sentient body and sentient soul, which are a unity. From our standpoint we can indeed see that here, in a certain sense, like things are meeting from both sides. The "I" comes from the one side and has directed itself upon itself, thus bringing the world of pure thought up to the not-"I"; in other words, all the laws of thought that are expressed in logic. Sense impressions come from the other side. If now we would really present the not-"I" that expresses itself here as it is for the not-"I," then we must say that sensory impression is simply direction upon oneself, which here, however, proceeds from the not-"I." The sensory impression surely consists precisely of this: a part of the not-"I"—the part of corporeity we were compelled to call the finest elaboration of the not-"I," since it bears within it the possibility of the "I"—can direct itself upon the whole corporeal world. The human body, which is a sense organ throughout its entire surface (with only slight exception), is an apparatus wherein the world is reflected—the not-"I" to which itself belongs. The human body can even reflect itself within itself, yielding thereby the best expression for the peculiar reflexive process of the not-"I." By its very sensory activity it provides the possibility of the "I" being kindled in thought. Thus, in sensory activity, too, we have something that exists itself, and with this we see the standard for reality that derives from the "I" applied to the not-"I." Accordingly, therefore, we have the meeting of like things, since both factors come about through a kind of reflexive activity—pure thought on the one side and *pure perception* on the other. The fact that here like things do indeed meet can also be made clear to us by means of the following considerations, which may be said to furnish a test for the foregoing thoughts.

Sensory perception surveys the whole fullness of the world of senses. So-called sense objects appear there to naive sensory perception. From that perspective, however, the fact is disregarded that each object represents a certain sum of individual sensory portions that are first unified by thought. Now, once thought consciously immerses itself in the world of senses, the objects are dissolved, so to speak, into separate sensory perceptions, such as red, bright, warm, loud, fine, firm, and so on. Now if pure thought probes the nature of those phenomenal forms of the not-"I" further, it finds that all these sensory qualities, and with them the objects they form, are nothing but concepts, which are nonetheless given in a way very different from the concepts created by the "I" in thinking.

Whereas thought—or rather the individual concepts themselves—do not denote reality in themselves but only when comprehended in the pure "I," we now find these same concepts given from the side of the not-"I" in a way that is independent of the "I," precisely by pure perception. Therefore, such concepts—which the "I" does not merely create from the sum of all conceptual possibility but *finds again* in percepts—are the real objects or, generally, the realities of the not-"I." When pure thought and pure perception meet, the "I" and not-"I" can reunite, which leads to cognition. With this we have found the epistemological significance of perception.

The path to knowledge (merely sketched here in broad outline) is actually applied in all natural research, where it keeps strictly within its province; we find that this process belongs to all the activities of nature. Both the growth of human beings to the "I" and knowledge of nature are similar processes; they have a great significance in cosmic events. We may look with awe at nature's activities, whose shaping forces create the precondition for the "I." In awe, we may also direct the pure thoughts given to us by nature acting on pure sensory experience. Such awe is needed to continue correctly the process of world-becoming through knowledge of nature. That awe involves recognizing the fact that we ourselves are only part of the great becoming—that we, as

"I," must feel a part of the not-"I," that the things surrounding us are our fellow human beings, who are in their own way beings like ourselves. Then our striving for knowledge becomes a search by our spirit, our "I," for the spirit—the "I"—of phenomena.

Here we have one side of the relationship between "I" and not-"I" that leads to sensory perception and so to knowledge of nature. It is the side on which the "I" applies its standard of reality to the not-"I."

There is also another side that leads to the higher "I" that receives its reality from the not-"I." This is the path to initiation, or suprasensory perception—that is, to higher knowledge and reality. In principle, of course, nothing is changed in the concept of perception as previously developed, whether we are dealing with sensory or suprasensory perception. That this second side is extremely important becomes clear from the fact that knowledge of nature, while it creates a balance between "I" and not-"I," does so only as a stage on the path to complete unity. In knowledge, the "I" does indeed return, so to speak, pure thought to nature, but it retains its own living being for itself; to itself it remains severed from the not-"I." Hence, too, knowledge of pure thought often seems to us cold and hostile to life. Warmth and life come to this knowledge from the feeling and certainty that the stage of pure thought signifies only the first step toward true unity with the not-"I."

It cannot be our purpose here to describe the path to the higher worlds, but only to point out, based on epistemological considerations, that such a path to higher knowledge does exist. It is true that such a path at the beginning indicates a sacrifice that the "I" must make. At the same time, we also find as our goal the attainment of a new and higher self that exists in the not-"I." Through initiation, human beings apprehend the world outwardly from within; we penetrate forward to the shaping forces hidden in nature's activities and to the "I" of nature as a whole. This is the grand perspective that opens up before us when we carry the theory of knowledge to its correct conclusion. Moreover, in the development of a new and higher "I," we have a process enacted in the not-"I." However, whereas the parallel process in the activity of the senses is accomplished by the shaping forces of existence without the human help, this second process must be brought about by human beings themselves. Here we attain a true creative share in the "world process." This comes about through a sacrifice of the lower self, but that sacrifice is simply our answer to the sacrifice of the shaping forces of existence when we were created through our "I." Through initiation human beings return to the ruling powers what they sacrificed to produce them.

After everything we have reflected upon, it should not be difficult to grasp this thought, since our whole theory of knowledge leads us to apprehend the severance of the "I" from the not-"I" as a spiritual process—that is, as a process behind which there are conscious forces, because no consciousness could otherwise form itself as the result of this process. Nevertheless, the "I" is spirit, consciousness, and reality, and it incorporates from the whole consciousness of the not-"I." The path to higher knowledge is shown to us by Spiritual Science; from higher worlds it brings down to humankind what will enable it in the future to develop the higher "I." Once we have become familiar with the idea that in the case of the higher worlds we are not dealing with abstractions, but rather with powers and beings above humankind and of whose spirit the human "I" is a spark, then we can understand that with the principle of the "I"-development we have apprehended a world principle of development.

Three times we saw how something higher is shaped when a force directs itself toward itself. The not-"I," which directs itself upon itself in sensory activity, is the first development, as it were, of the "I." Pure perception arises from this, and with it the possible kindling of the human "I." The second development of the "I" is in observation of thought. Third, the pure "I" offers the possibility that the higher self may be formed by the "I" giving back to the not-"I" all the spirituality it had taken from it. If we may presuppose this human capacity today, we must still acknowledge that this capacity was once conferred on humankind from higher worlds by supra-human beings. Moreover, without going beyond outer historical facts, we can point to the moment when this happened.

If we compare the conditions of our own culture and consciousness with those of pre-Christian civilizations, we can see how the emergence of intellectual self-awareness, independence, and individualism makes itself gradually felt from the earlier group-consciousness of national uniformity. The greatest "I" development, we can say, is at this turning point of human development, and we can struggle through to acknowledge that it is essentially true to say that what was with God in the beginning and from which all that was made became flesh at the beginning of our era, when the spirit of humankind, from which the growth to the "I" developed, directed itself upon itself. Through this, the higher self of all humankind arose as the Christ spirit, who gave the first impulse and possibility for the individual human beings, through their own free sacrificial gift, to hand on the great, grand sacrifice.

This is described for us by Spiritual Science, and it may spur us on the path it points toward if we are able through the self-perception of our own spirit to develop the ideas that can lead us to an understanding of these lofty principles.

2

Natural Science and Spiritual Science

Those who have decided to allow epistemological considerations to have a determining influence on their views quickly find themselves compelled to extend such considerations to long-familiar and unquestioned concepts, so that eventually all aspects of their worldviews are informed by circumspection. It should be noted in this connection that the need for epistemological circumspection first makes itself felt when we have reached some stage or other of "knowledge," and it does not leave us until we have succeeded in reconciling the newly won area of knowledge with the general principles of epistemology.

Any worldview must eventually take such a path if it wishes to withstand its own scrutiny. The more deeply any worldview seeks to penetrate the nature of reality, the more difficult it will be to attain epistemological circumspection in every aspect. We find then that it is not enough to adhere in a general way to certain fundamental principles, but that the important point is how exactly to apply such principles, because the character of a worldview will depend on this. It will certainly be clear that epistemological principles must not in any way be colored by the particular worldview whose foundations they will form, although the path along which such principles are discovered leads backward from knowledge to the foundations. The fact is that what we must do when looking back in this way is to lift into consciousness what, by acquiring knowledge, we had unconsciously used as our foundation, impelled by an urge for knowledge.

Now, if a worldview comes into question, such as Spiritual Science or Anthroposophy (which claims most comprehensively to embrace all the right apperceptions contained in other worldviews), if we then follow Spiritual Science, we not only need to be able to base the teachings of Spiritual Science on an epistemology, but we must also show—using particular characteristics in the use of the general epistemological principles—how the various worldviews are brought about. We may assume that such contacts with other worldviews will automatically arise if we rightly and conscientiously submit to the epistemological discipline of Spiritual Science, but here again we will see that we must first have a comprehensive grasp of Spiritual Science before we can retrospectively form a true approximation of the other views of the universe. When it is said, therefore, that Spiritual Science subsumes in itself such true knowledge as the other worldviews contain, we must not conversely believe that by simply putting individual worldviews, based on the perspectives of natural science, philosophy, religion, and perhaps of art together we will gain a picture of Spiritual Science. Spiritual Science must be understood through itself. We know from spiritual investigators that it is not just an aggregate of doctrines but also the way to life in the spirit; it is our task to bring our awareness into harmony with it right where we stand, and by clothing itself in our categories of knowledge, it also provides the means of doing this. A theory of knowledge is intended to give us firm inner support and to show us the threads that join us to the opinions of other human beings and to life as a whole.

Chapter 1, "The 'I' and the Nature of the Human Being," shows, above all, how followers of Spiritual Science have a particular need to base their consciousness on an epistemological foundation. Now we attempt—based on the general epistemological principles emerging in this little treatise—to present the several areas of Spiritual Science in a system of ideas adapted to today's normal capacity for knowledge. Now, one may argue that such an attempt would press the vital spirituality of our science into dry categories of thought. Such an objection would be perfectly justified if we wished to use the concepts of everyday thinking. We do not need, however, to lapse into the error of dead abstractionism but will address ourselves to the vital spring of spirituality that exists in every human being. Indeed, the object of chapter 1 is to uncover the spring that is clogged up today in most people. Therefore, the following reflections are offered as a structure of brief summaries based on the epistemological foundations contained therein.

We expect a worldview to explain the relationship between the world and our consciousness. If we want to know the nature of the world "in itself," we must ask this question: What is the world for us? If it is possible for the world to be for us as it exists "in itself," any certainty of this must come from ourselves. Thus, all striving for knowledge begins in the "I." The "I" must discover its own reality within itself and then apply that reality as a standard to the not-"I," or the world. Thus it is that the "I" comes to oppose itself at the outset in all its purity to the not-"I." Therefore, everything derived from the not-"I" must be eliminated from the "I"—beginning with all impressions, perceptions, sensations, and feelings, then all thoughts that recall the not-"I." All that is left is pure "I" as the sum of pure thoughts—in other words, the faculty for creating logical and mathematical forms. If we now examine the nature of those forms (observation of thought), the "I" finds its own essence as the concept of the concept. This is, as indeed is also observation of thought, a form that has its own essence for content, carried by its own form.

With this, we have found the standard for what we sought—that is, reality. In the process of "I" apprehension, we see how the pure "I" articulates itself from the not-"I," and thus we can determine three stages in the natural relationship between "I" and not-"I." We find the stage of separation; the stage of equilibrium between the two, at which the "I" is present only insofar as it derives its content from the not-"I"; and the stage at which the "I" is present in the not-"I" only as potential. We may designate these three stages as the human spirit, soul, and body. Striving for knowledge indicates an effort of the "I" to consummate its reunion with the not-"I." The "I" seeks to attain this, first, by applying its standard of reality to the not-"I" through pure thought. This is possible at the point where the "I" began to free itself from the not-"I." The expression for that point is sensory perception, which we must now see as self-direction of the not-"I" itself, in that the senses, a part of the not-"I," reflect the outer world in a way similar to when the "I" emerges pure through thought directing itself upon itself. Hence, if like meets like—pure perception and pure thought—knowledge is the result.

Now, before we pursue the epistemological thread further, let us more clearly demarcate the sphere to which the epistemological method as defined applies. Everything accessible to our senses constitutes the objects of this mode of observation—the material world, in which the human body is the foremost object. The human body opens access to that world for us, and a simple reflection will show us that it holds everything in itself that the material world signifies. We like to divide the sensory world into various realms of nature, and we designate such knowledge "natural science."

We must note carefully that natural science acts correctly by limiting itself to phenomena accessible to our senses. Nonetheless, it is also clear that the methods of natural science, developed on the basis of sensory perception by pure thought, cannot succeed when investigating the two other principal constituents of the human being (soul and spirit), because they withhold themselves from sensory perception. Just as we see that the material human body essentially constitutes the method and matter of the natural-scientific view, likewise the soul indicates the means and the object of the religious view, and only Spiritual Science has the power to present the human spirit as its basis. Now, because the human spirit immerses itself in the bodily world and in contemplating nature, whereas the soul forms the connecting link between body and spirit, we can understand how only Spiritual Science would have the power to solve the mysteries of existence. On the other hand, we recognize that our best approach to Spiritual Science and its perspective is a quick survey of the world of sensory perception, which allows us to shed light on the question of how far the beings of nature speak to our senses, and whether we can, in doing so, detect anything that eludes sensory observation.

We can quickly determine that what exists immediately before the senses is simply a sum of sensory qualities. Moreover, our ability to distinguish among the realms of nature does not come about on the strength of pure perception. On the one hand, we must apprehend sensory perceptions as a primal expression of the not-"I," on which the "I" does not exert the slightest influence, while on the other hand we have to apply pure thought to these sensory perceptions. Thus we must shed light on how human beings make such distinctions within sensory perceptions through the natural application of their faculty of knowledge.

Natural science has recorded great successes in regard to the so-called mineral world, the "inanimate." Since we encounter this mineral element in contemplating all objects of sensory perception, we can easily understand why natural-scientific worldviews tend to trace sensory phenomena back to the mineral element. Now we need to examine how this is an error. Scrutinizing carefully, whatever remains unchanged to thinking that firmly confronts sensory perception we call mineral, or inanimate. The term *mineral* refers to the part of the sensible world that does not change on its own, but requires a stimulus from without to change in a way this is wholly perceptible to the senses. Such a reaction is in complete agreement with the inherently changeless laws of logic that allow the pure "I" to grasp the sensory world. Such agreement shouldn't surprise us if we realize that, when pure perception encounters pure thought, elements wholly of the same kind can unite. Here, too, we find the reason that natural scientists, when contemplating the world, feel a need to trace the whole world of perception—even the spiritual world—back to relationships in the mineral realm. The laws of nature express this agreement; such laws are apprehended subjectively in thought and formulated in universal language, and are found again objectively in the world of senses and actualized in the individual instance.

To express the inherent immutability of the mineral world, natural science uses the concept of matter, defined as the bearer of perceived sensory qualities. The error in viewing matter as something that actually exists has often been exposed; it is enough to point out that sensory qualities must always be assigned to matter or to atoms that are thought of as equally real in order to characterize them, so that for this reason (if for no other) they are unfit to be taken as a true basis for sensory perceptions. Nevertheless, apart from this, the reality of matter—atoms and molecules, even electrons—has in recent times melted away, as it were, in the hands of natural science itself.

Even when we examine the concept of motion—which has an application in all areas of modern physics—we do not go beyond the realm of sensory qualities, regardless of whether we accept motion as the basis of cosmic ether or electrons; though divested precisely of the characteristic importance of "matter," they are revealed by their very capacity for motion as elements perceptible to the senses. It is just this concept of motion that allows us to see most clearly that reducing sensory qualities to something objectively real and unchanging is not valid.

If we accept motion not as a general concept but as an actual phenomenon—that is, as motion that actually occurs—we become clearly aware that we are dealing with sensory elements related to light and, accordingly, to the sense of sight. Though appropriate here, we must reserve our discussion of space for a later chapter. We will note only that it is precisely the most modern physicists and mathematicians who adduce the physiology of the eye to explain the origin of space as an idea. It might be thought that the so-called sense of touch likewise plays a part in the production of the idea of motion. This would be incorrect; the sense of touch instead apprehends the moments of rest, from which only an objectively reasoned inference leads us to motion.

Now, when natural science feels it needs to trace the complicated phenomena of the sense-perceptible world back to motions, it thus acknowledges that perceptions of light are more trustworthy than any other sensory perceptions. Indeed, that fact has general application for natural science, whose theories, one would say, are based exclusively on visual perceptions—that is, perceptions of light. One cannot object to referring perceptions of sound to motion, inasmuch as sound phenomena can be made accessible to the eye. On the other hand, it is not logically possible to refer phenomena of light to motions; in doing so, we are certainly not abandoning the area of light perception to enter a more universal field. Surely, we may not assume that the explanation is the very thing we wish to explain. Just as it is inadmissible to trace thought, by means of thoughts, back to something else, likewise it is not valid to base light on phenomena of motion. In this sense, we encounter Goethe's saying, so surprising to modern consciousness: "Light is the simplest, most undivided and homogeneous essence known to us. It is not a compound."

Now we can say that natural-scientific knowledge proceeds on the basis of light perceptions and pure thought. Thus, we must recognize two things in light perception and pure thought that correlate immediately, in full accordance, with our theory of knowledge, which led us to conclude that, when pure perception and pure thought meet, there is a mingling of absolutely like elements. Here we find it established precisely that one sensory perception—that of light—corresponds directly to thought. Here, however, we have an immediate relationship between the sense perceptible and the suprasensory, which can be formulated: *Pure thought is the suprasensory element in light, or light is the sense-perceptible expression of pure thought.*

It would be interesting to ask whether, similarly, we can find a directly corresponding suprasensory thing for the other sensory phenomena, since for pure thought they are accessible only indirectly through light perceptions. However, only Spiritual Science will be suitable for this, as we are still dealing with considerations of natural science. Spiritual Science shows us, in fact, that behind tone, for example, there is still something essentially different from simple movement phenomena in the air. Thus, we see how there is already a mingling of a sensory and a suprasensory thing in all intellectual knowledge based on the senses. With this, a connection with Spiritual Science becomes apparent to us. If we wish to describe the mineral kingdom within the world of perception, we must look for an expression of the part of the perceptual world that remains unchanged for pure thought. As we saw, not all designations are admissible for a material content of the mineral kingdom, so let us say tentatively that the mineral kingdom can be analyzed for intellectual consideration as a sum of mineral (physical, chemical, etc.) forces. Here, force does not mean something that causes or carries the mineral properties, but the mineral phenomena themselves, in both their sensory and suprasensory connection. Now we can ask this question: Can we find even more forms of force within the perceived world?

Now, if we move on to the sense-perceptible phenomena we call the plant kingdom, the first thing we meet again is the mineral forces, though in a far more complex interrelationship.

For us, this is expressed in such a way that a perceptual complex called *oxygen* is the same whether obtained from the mineral kingdom or from artificial or natural processes in the plant world. With such investigations, of course, we only touch the mineral part of the plant—that is, the part that remains unchanged before strict thought. However, this is the case only when the plant lacks precisely what makes it a plant; in a "living" plant, we see that the mineral does not remain unchanged before strict thought. We must allow a changeable element into the rigid laws of logic to touch the essence of the plant. That element is expressed in the concept of development, or growth, in contrast to the purely logical concept of being.

In a later section of our epistemological investigations of Spiritual Science (which deal only with being), we will examine how far the concept of development must be set above the forms of logic. Here it is enough to note that, through the concept of development, we express the fact that, in the case of the plant we can see, precisely with respect to mineralogy, it does not remain unchanged before purely logical thought. We see the plant grow, nourish, and propagate itself—that is, we notice a change that is not, as with the mineral, caused externally, but within the plant itself. The external conditions (sunshine, rain, suitable soil, etc.) merely provide an opportunity, enabling the mineral element, which needs external influences, to follow the causes in the plant itself that produce changes. We see that the mineral element in the plant in no way follows its proper laws, but contrasts with its ordinary behavior. This may be seen, surely, from the fact that the plant's mineral structure is destroyed at once by external influences when the counteraction of the plant ceases. We clearly see that we are confronted with a new kind of force that differs fundamentally from the mineral forces. Such forces prove stronger than the mineral forces and overcome them. In the life forms of plants, we see those forces expressed; for their own ends, they convert the mineral forces into a garment to veil themselves. Regarding plants, we may speak of corporeality in which the suprasensory plant nature lives.

Again, we see the contact with Spiritual Science, which describes a suprasensory part of the plant for us. That part Spiritual Science calls the *etheric body,* and because material concepts are inevitably easily attached to this term in spite of everything, it is important that we learn to visualize clearly the true nature of the etheric body of plants based on the strength of natural-scientific considerations. If the designation of matter as the bearer of the mineral properties cannot be admitted in the mineral world, this is even more so with regard to plant activity. Indeed, we are stuck with material concepts insofar as we persist in applying purely logical forms of thinking without the fluid element of development to the plant kingdom. However, from this schematic treatment of natural philosophy the concept of the cell also arose as a materially objective representative of the life processes. Although we can use the word *cell,* we must at the same time note what is actually given—a force center of a higher order within the mineral world of our perception. We are confronted by two kinds of forces in the sensory presentation of plants and, correspondingly, of animals and human beings: mineral forces and plant forces. Now, if we observe that those plant forces pervade all organic life and are present wherever we can speak of a cell system, we can say that the etheric body is the sum of the forces that make minerals into cells. In terms of sensory perception, the expression of the suprasensory etheric body is in the forms of the plant that develop through growth, maintain themselves through nutrition, and transmit themselves through propagation.

If we move on to the animal kingdom, we see the corporeality of the animal again subject to the influence of new forces that essentially differ from plant forces. This is expressed not only in the mineral structure of the animal, but also in its life history. Whereas we see the plant bound to the soil that surrounds it—its mineral structure is destroyed if the plant is torn from the soil in which it grows—we see that the animal detaches itself from its mother earth without the mineral structure being destroyed. Thus, these new forces in turn show themselves stronger than the preceding ones, and they make the mineral formation even more complicated. They add to the expression of the etheric body—to the relatively simple cellular structure of plants—a system of glands that controls the circulation of fluids in the organism. This organism is no longer united with the mother soil, as is the plant. These forces incorporate with the whole a new system, which is the perceptible expression of those new forces. In their nature, the forces themselves are "inward." They give the animal the mobility it needs, having separated from the mother soil—for example, for nutrition—and they reestablish a connection between the animal and the outer world.

This new assemblage is the nervous system, a perceptible expression of inwardness. The nerves lead outer impression inward through the sense organs, while they lead the internal impulses outward through the organs of movement. When we note the fact that these forces are present wherever the effects of inner nature manifest, we get a picture of the new force body, much in the way that we saw previously in the case of the etheric body, and with this we have a definition for the suprasensory aspect of animals and human beings that Spiritual Science calls the *sentient body,* or *astral body.* The sentient body is the sum of the forces that make cells into nerves.

Having thoroughly explored the world of corporeality with the help of an epistemologically defensible natural-scientific method, it becomes our obvious task to connect the human body with this train of thought. We find the human body to be a mineral structure, shaped by life forces, and illumined with consciousness by the forces of subjectivity. We can distinguish with the terms *physical body, etheric body,* and *astral body,* but these are modified by a fourth kind of force that, continuing our previous definitions, we can describe as follows. The human body is distinguished from an animal body by a sum of forces that links the nerve substance together to form the human brain; surely, there can be no doubt that in the structure and size of the brain we have the corporeal difference between human beings and the highest animals, whatever attitude we may otherwise adopt about the relationship between animals and human beings.

However, we must not view the new form of forces we are discussing here as we have thus far. In these structures we no longer have an expression of corporeality in the sense that thought stands in contrast to their sensory manifestation. Rather, here we have to deal with the sense-perceptible expression of thought itself. Nor can we continue to distinguish between ourselves and the suprasensory aspects of those phenomena, because we are ourselves that sum of forces. We find this sum of forces as a being—the "I"—from which the standard for the whole of natural scientific inquiry was taken. These new forces can alone apprehend themselves as the theory of knowledge. In observation of thinking, we apprehend the suprasensory directly. Only Spiritual Science can have a place in this extension of the natural sciences. Thus, the theory of knowledge foreshadowed at the beginning leads us, by its application as a natural science, to the very boundary of Spiritual Science.

Now we can take up the thread of our epistemological considerations that we let drop in the chapter, "The 'I' and the Nature of the Human Being." The "I" apprehends itself in itself as reality. Before it could base itself upon itself, it had to separate itself from the not-"I." Natural-scientific knowledge arises through the "I," with its most essential nature, pure thought, reaching out to the not-"I," where it finds sensory perception, the most essential expression of the not-"I." Nevertheless, there is yet another area in which the "I" is found in an intimate natural union with the not-"I." The expression for this is the human soul, and we succeeded in deriving its threefold nature as sentient soul, intellectual soul, and consciousness soul from the subtler relationships between "I" and the not-"I."

Now that we have explored the areas of the not-"I," we find that there we have to deal with three different kinds of forces, with which the fourth form, the "I," now can maintain a connection. In this way, we reach to a new understanding of the characteristic differences of the three aspects of the soul, since we see that the "I" has a natural connection with each of the three realms of force. We can convince ourselves of this truth and once more achieve a particularly intimate contact with Spiritual Science by reflecting that it is we ourselves who, in a suprasensory way, are placed within the forces of nature's realms, so that we are thus directly experiencing that connection from the side of the "I." The sphere thus indicated, the human soul, is characterized by the concept of the personal and unique; it effects the junction between the universality of pure thought and the singularity of sensory perceptions, but the issue here is not the thoughts we gain about the sensory world, since they belong to natural-scientific knowledge, but the way the "I" has its being amid outer nature.

We know the human bodily organization— the part of the not-"I" that includes the possibility of the "I"—as a mineral structure, formed and maintained by life forces, unfolded to the outside world by forces of subjectivity. It is an apparatus that possesses the capacity for sensation through the sense organs, and through the organs of motion the capability of action. It should be noted that neither sensation nor action become facts by virtue of that apparatus alone. The fourth kind of force, the "I," is needed for this—to use or activate the apparatus. Because the possibility of sensation and action originates with the astral body, it is a union of the "I" and the forces of the astral body that we experience as sensation or immediate urge. Insofar as the "I" lives by the forces of the astral body, it is sensation, or sentient soul. By using the term *sensation,* we are designating the inner experience that unites with an external sense impression. However, the stimuli to action that follow directly from the sensations are also part of the sphere of the sentient soul.

The next area of the unique, or personal, will have to be described according to what the "I" experiences with the forces of the etheric body. Consider once more the sensations; they are the subjective experiences of the sensory qualities. Those experiences are wholly chaotic, without any relationships. One experience is worth the same as any other; the important point to note is that such an experience is completely ended when the sense organ in question turns away, or the outer stimulus ceases. Nothing is left over if we merely regard the sensation;

other forces are needed to retain anything of the sensations. Such forces, in fact, do exist—the forces of the etheric body with which the "I" is now able to unite. However, since the "I" is connected with the outside world only through the senses—that is, through the forces of the astral body—it can utilize the forces of the etheric body only insofar as the astral body supplies the material for this. The forces of the etheric body are organizing, formative forces; if the "I" unites them with the chaos of sensations, experiences will present themselves to the "I," in which the sensations are cast into forms, retained, coordinated, and distinguished. The "I," with the help of the etheric body's forces, transforms sensations into mental images. Mental images are the remains of all that the "I" experiences in the outer world, even after the sensations have ceased. All phenomena of memory are connected with this area of inner experience, comprehensively styled the intellectual soul. The intellectual soul is the "I" insofar as the "I" is united to the forces of the etheric body. Accordingly, the stimuli to action that originate in the faculty of memory—habits, inclinations, passions, and so on—belong to this sphere.

At this point we wish to counter the argument that the definitions of sensation, mental image, instinct, habit, and so on apply also to animals, and even to plants. There is a widespread tendency today—when molecular memory, atomic soul, and so on are current expressions—to study the beings of nature not in their typical appearances, but in the "transition forms." The first thing to be said about this is that such distinctions among mineral, plant, and animal refer to the body of those beings. Here, however, we are concerned with the soul, the human soul, the only one about which our present means enable us to affirm anything. In a subsequent discussion, once we have laid the necessary foundations, we will be able discuss also the soul-spiritual aspect of the natural kingdoms. It is true that we will then see that we are justified in ascribing to the animals after their kind a sentient soul and, to the higher species, even traces of an intellectual soul, but only by setting out from the animal "I," which differs fundamentally from the human.

Now, if the "I" unites further with the forces of the physical body, it has taken complete possession of its whole corporeal organization. With this, we enter the sphere of uniqueness in which the "I," by virtue of its sensations, mental images and experiences, is able to develop its universality. The mental images become concepts; the "I," within its mineral body, can feel separated from the outer world, and we gain the contrast of "I" and not-"I," which formed the beginning of our epistemological considerations. Whereas human consciousness (insofar as sentient and intellectual souls are concerned) depends on external stimuli, it now becomes self-aware. Spiritual Science calls that area of uniqueness the consciousness soul. The area of activity that corresponds to the consciousness soul is morality. In the consciousness soul, we attain moral independence, whereby we allow own ideals to flow out into the world through our actions. We see that the natural conjunction between "I" and not-"I" has two forms of expression, which lead to independence in the consciousness soul—independence of knowledge and independence of action. We can also classify action according to three points of view—that is, according to the path it takes within the threefold sphere of uniqueness. It is the "I" that acts, but moral independence can be achieved only after the "I" has apprehended itself in independence.

With this, we have now established contact with Spiritual Science on the side of action. This is extremely important, because it shows us that the entry to spirituality begins with an action no less than with an act of knowledge. Action and knowledge coincide. Insofar as apprehending the "I" appears as the culmination of natural science, it is knowledge; as action wholly within the spiritual sphere, it is the entry to spiritual worlds. Through sensory and soul life, human beings depend on the forces of nature; by apprehending the "I," human beings take their place among the creative beings of the world.

Now, if we look back at the path that the "natural application of our faculty of knowledge"—the application of natural scientific methods—has won for us, we see that we can now distinguish among the realms of nature, because we ourselves, as "I"-beings, are in natural union with those "fields of force"; hence, the distinction between, and a doctrine of, the natural realms can be built on the reality of the "I." Such a classification then contains nothing arbitrary or accidental, but we find in it at various stages the reality of spiritual life to which the "I" as a self-aware spirit belongs. The concepts we have formed are not dead abstractions, otherwise we should never have established a connection with spiritual-scientific investigations. We had to overcome the dead, mineral-like logic and let living concepts grow from the concept of the concept, the pure "I," which is living, spiritual reality. Nevertheless, we have achieved something more than that. By our circular progress, from basing cognitive "I"-knowledge by applying it to the realms of nature and back to the "I," we have forged a ring of confidence in the results of Spiritual Science. That takes us another step; now we are also in a position to understand the other side of cognition, the spiritual-scientific one, not only in terms of theory, but also in terms of method.

When the "I" as consciousness soul becomes aware of its creative force, it will also be prepared to advance to spiritual action; we will thus decide to enter the path shown to us by Spiritual Science. In knowledge-as-theory, it appears as the path of self-denial, or sacrifice, with a scarcely discerned goal; in knowledge as action we can now take that first step, with a clear purpose, in the direction that the spiritual teacher indicates.

We may recognize that higher knowledge is possible from the formulation of the theory of our intellectual knowledge (outlined in the preceding chapter). If the "I" in intellectual knowledge applies its standard of reality to the not-"I," it is just one of three possibilities. We must acknowledge that a further stage of knowledge is possible if we envisage the fact that now the "I" no longer preponderates in the relations between the two factors, "I" and not-"I," but that both are in equilibrium (imaginative knowledge). The possibility of a third stage is furnished by the view that the not-"I" now predominates and provides the standard for a new reality—the "I," the higher self (inspired knowledge). Now, if the essence of knowledge involves the "I" achieving reunification with the not-"I," from which it had detached itself, we find that the difference between the intellectual and the other stages of knowledge consists of the intellect accomplishing that reunion in a more theoretical way, by the "I" returning pure thought to the not-"I," as it were; but to reach the higher knowledge, the "I," in its living spirituality, we must approach the not-"I" by practical means. The spiritual investigator's testimony leads us from recognizing the possibility of higher knowledge to recognizing its reality, and the confidence in the spiritual investigator's testimony—won in the process of intellectual knowledge—leads us further to an understanding of the path to spiritual investigation, and finally on to that path itself.

The area of action for intellectual knowledge is sensory experience, the impressions that the "I" receives from the not-"I" when it remains placed in opposition to it. Now, where do we find the area of action for the path to higher knowledge? Clearly in the interactions between "I" and not-"I," by which both are united inwardly.

We see clearly that the sphere of action for the "I" on the path to higher knowledge is the human soul. As we saw, the soul in its threefold structure is the area of human nature where the "I" participates directly in the life of the not-"I." However, whereas the soul in natural life transmits the message sent by the not-"I" as a corporeal sensory impression, that process must now suffer a reversal; whereas the "I" is a recipient in intellectual knowledge, it must be a giver on the path to higher knowledge. It must pour its purest essence into the not-"I"—that is, primarily into the sphere of the not-"I" in which the "I" already participates: in the soul. From this perspective, if we consider the directions given by the spiritual teacher, we discover how this reversal takes place; we find in this reversal a means to the action of the "I" on the soul, and there is no recess of the soul that is not affected by that work.

When it is shown how the "I" must make itself entirely insensitive to impressions of the senses and how consciousness must empty itself of every sensory remnant to fill itself with content deriving from the spirit, then we see how the reversal in the relationships between "I" and not-"I" is affected. Meditation is the name given to that state, and the "I" must execute that work with a strong will. As a result, we are given a description of how the "I" gradually advances to the spiritual springs from which it flowed. To enlarge on further details is, of course, beyond the scope of a treatise such as this. The "I" cannot enter the path by proxy, but there is one effect that such considerations should have; the path to higher knowledge will be made intelligible and its significance made familiar to us.

Thus, we reach a standpoint in regard to life that is characterized by the work on the soul intended to lead to reuniting the "I" with its prime source, what we call the *Divine*. That perspective toward life may be called religion, if we take the word in its proper sense. We laid it out to begin with that the soul signifies the way and the object of a religious mode of contemplation. Now, having arrived at a truly religious standpoint with regard to life, we can also come to understand the nature of a perspective that is still religious, though unconscious, as well as understanding the significance of the historical "religions."

We find it confirmed that, by discovering an epistemological basis for the teachings of Spiritual Science, we can also discover the basis for other worldviews. We can show no greater respect for natural science than by using its method. That will bring us into harmony with others who desire truth exclusively in the field of natural science and whose spiritual being does not gain confidence in its own spiritual reality and, therefore, confidence in the reality of spiritual-scientific investigations. Looking back from our religious standpoint, we will also feel united with others whose desire for a life in the spirit does not dare to look its own spirit in the face—those who, to avoid the union with the divine in religious surrender cannot decide to seek, through Spiritual Science in self-awareness, reunion with the Divine.

If we learn to appreciate the value of other worldviews in this way, we owe it to Spiritual Science—whose doctrines lie before us, summoning us rightly to use the forces of knowledge we already possess, giving us the courage to base ourselves on our own spiritual nature, and thereby releasing our forces for life in the spirit for knowledge as deed.

3

The Philosophy of Contradiction

We have become so familiar with the contradictions of life and the human soul that we tend to speak of them as permanent aspects of our worldview. All presentations of life and, the artistic ones above all, are fond of using this motif. Yet, on close examination, such presentations and expositions of contradictions serve to unify them on a higher plane, whether in scientific synthesis or in artistic transfiguration. Although we may delight greatly in contemplating our colorful and self-contradictory life in all its variety, and although we may feel strongly that life is constantly assuming new shapes to annihilate itself, we nevertheless have the need—with regard to a scientific interpretation of life and the universe—for a "system" not to include contradiction.

It may give us pause that materialistic monism,[1] as a coherent, self-consistent explanation of the cosmos, should be so prevalent today, when contradictions in the life of individuals and nations impress themselves upon us so powerfully as

---

[1] Spiritual monism is the ontological position that there is only one kind of being, that this being is spirit, that all spirit is eternal, and that material objects merely appear to exist. —ED.

a reality. Behind the "monistic" natural philosophy is the thought that natural laws are the basis of all processes and that any contradictions are illusions that must vanish as our understanding grows. Anthroposophy, or Spiritual Science, appears filled with contradictions compared to a view such as spiritual monism. Viewed from this perspective, the first two chapters of this epistemological foundation to a Spiritual Science will undoubtedly seem unacceptable, since they openly and explicitly use the greatest contradictions. This offers us sufficient reason to turn our attention to the nature of contradiction and try to follow, in brief outline, the nature of non-contradictory thought to justify the contradictions contained in those chapters.

The desire not to suffer contradictions in scientific thinking is so strong that a doctrine exists that may be called "the law of non-contradiction." This doctrine is logic, which is usually traced back to a few principles that, similar to mathematical axioms, are intended to be neither susceptible to nor in need of further proof. Seeing that contradictory thought is called "false," and non-contradictory thought called "true," it would be most interesting for us to find out which axiom expresses this. To indicate what should be considered false or true, logic enunciates the axiom of non-contradiction. As formulated by Aristotle, the originator of logic, it says, "One cannot say of something that it is and that it is not in the same respect and at the same time."[2] This is usually expressed symbolically thus: The two judgments, A is B and A is not B, cannot both be true

---

2   The three classical laws: 1) *the law of identity* (every thing is the same with itself and different from another); 2) *the law of non-contradiction;* and 3) *the law of excluded middle* (there cannot be an intermediate between contradictories, but of one subject we must either affirm or deny any one predicate). See Aristotle, *Metaphysics,* book 4.

at the same time. The content of that axiom is negative; it characterizes what is false. Therefore, if we obtain a proposition as the result of true thought, we should be precluded from reaching its opposite by true thought, as well.

In fact, however, cases are well known in which, for equally sound logical reasons, two propositions can be presented, each of which asserts the contrary of the other. Such propositions are termed *antinomies*. One of the best-known antinomies states that reason demands that there will be a first cause of all occurrences that are conditioned by nothing else, and that every cause in the world will be conditioned by one preceding it. One concludes from this "that we must abandon any assumption that the things and their relations are self-subsistent." Thus we see that the possibility of penetrating by reason the true grounds of existence is, in a certain sense, sacrificed to the axiom of non-contradiction, which is surely also a principle of that same reason. Would it not, then, be better for the present to question the axiom of non-contradiction as to whether it really possesses such absolute validity? Surely they are the same logical reasons that would subject reason to criticism, though they do lead to antinomies!

The first thing that must strike us about the axiom of non-contradiction is the principle of negation. It is clear that this principle is the most important in thought; it gives thought its basic character in terms of comparing and distinguishing. Here we may state that the principle of negation is not satisfied when we say that it is connected with the principle of affirmation, or positing, giving it as our reason that every negation presupposes a prior positing; for one might say with equal justification that every affirmation or positing must be preceded by the exclusion of all else. The primary concepts of thought themselves, true and false, condition one another, and the axiom of non-contradiction is the best example of the principle of negation being placed at the service of what is true. The axiom of non-contradiction, when one wishes to use it as a criterion of truth, immediately transforms itself into the axiom of the excluded third: Two mutually opposed judgments, A is B and A is not B, cannot both at the same time be false; a third judgment upon the same relationship between A and B is excluded; from the falsity of the one there follows the truth of the other. We can summarize both premises in one: A is either B or not B. In this formulation the second portion appears quite superfluous, for one easily comes to say that, if A is B, it cannot at the same time also not be B.

Surely it must be far more difficult to demonstrate the falsity of A is not B, for B is something wholly determinate, whereas not-B is no criterion whatever for A, and to demonstrate the falsity of not-B, all possible cases of not-B must be shown to be false. That we have a sufficient ground for the judgment A is B is far more important than the second portion of our formula. That is expressed by the axiom of the sufficient ground, which is shown here to be the most essential component of the axiom of non-contradiction. Now, if we are content not to characterize a sentence or concept that we express from the negative side, then we are left with the first half of our transformed axiom of non-contradiction: Once A (for sufficient reason!) has been designated as B, that must be definitive. However, that is the one essential principle of logic, the principle of identity that now contains in itself all other principles. It is incomprehensible how the principle of identity can sometimes be described today as absolutely void of content. It is clear that, if we want to probe the depth of the thought that leads to antinomies while wishing to avoid any contradiction (which, while obeying the same logical laws, declares itself incapable of reaching reality by its own strength), then we must cling to the principle of identity.

The principle of identity essentially says, "Every concept, every judgment is equal to itself." It is clear that we do not keep with the nature of that principle when we say that it requires us to understand the same presentment, the same concept, the same judgment on every occasion in the same way, since that would be merely a postulate of linguistic expression. The principle of identity must be understood wholly in terms of content. The content of a concept or judgment is fixed by it in the form that has once been posited. Every other meaning must remain expressly excluded, and that exclusion of everything else is already implied in that axiom. We do not need to stress it with a separate axiom. By that exclusion every contradiction, from the outset, is to be deprived of all support.

Logic understands well that there are various stages for exclusion, distinction, or negation. This is connected with the classification of concepts. An important distinction is that, according to subordinated, superordinated and coordinated concepts, several coordinated concepts are subordinated to one superordinated one. In this way there are entire conceptual series standing in a relation of sub-ordination—for example, lion, beast of prey, mammal, animate being, and so on. The axiom of identity appears self-evident wherever there is a question of diverse conceptual series. It is clear, for instance, that a chair is not a mammal. However, within the same conceptual series the principle of exclusion operates in such a way that two coordinated concepts that completely fill the concept superordinated to them exclude each other under any circumstances.

They are said to be contradictorily opposed to one another. If there are several coordinated concepts that must be subordinated to a superordinated one, their relationship is called a contrary opposition. An example of contradictory opposition is straight and crooked; the two concepts completely exhaust the superordinated concept of line. An example of contrary opposition is spring, summer, autumn, and winter for the superordinated concept of season. A line that is not straight must be crooked, but if it is not spring, it may be summer, autumn, or winter. Accordingly, the season of the year is not determined simply by the negation of spring. One must negate all the remaining contrarily opposed concepts to fix a definite concept of that same kind.

If we now compare a concept with what is super- or subordinated to it, we get a different relationship. The primary concern here is that the conceptual series should be properly formed, and we can gauge this by the fact that every concept must include all those superordinated to it in the same series. Thus, for instance, the previous series—lion, beast of prey, mammal, and so on—is formed incorrectly, since not all beasts of prey are mammals. The following is the correct series: lion, mammal, vertebrate, animal, living being. If we pick out any link from a correct series, we find all superordinated concepts contained in that one. It is true, of course, that it is the poorer by at least one characteristic.

If we analyze the concept mammal in the sense of the series, we find the concepts vertebrate, animal, living being, and so on contained in it. We saw that the coordinated concepts of a grade in the conceptual series exclude one another. The exclusion, however, does not extend to what is contained in all the coordinated concepts—the superordinated concept. The most important task of a conceptual science is to form correct series. In this sense, the principle of comparison, or inclusion, is as important as the principle of exclusion, or distinction. Thus we have a few general rules for the relatedness of concepts as applied to common logic. Most important, the principle of exclusion should be used in a rational way. We will now try to define the principle of exclusion more closely.

If the principle of identity is inherently justified, then any concept from its nature excludes what is other than itself. Whatever is excluded exists outside the concept and never enters it. That kind of exclusion isolates the individual concept in accordance with a definite, conceptually expressible viewpoint. It is the concept of side-by-side, in which nothing can ever step into the other's place without cancelling that other. That is the concept of space, which must be superordinated to all concepts and conceptual series that exclude each other, as the last and highest and, therefore, as common to them all, being contained in them. All individual series of concepts, to begin with, exclude one another in keeping with the principle of identity. So do all coordinated concepts of the same grade in a conceptual series, which nonetheless contain a common, superordinated concept. From every concept of a series, that series and no other leads upward, whereas downward, other series can be joined on—specifically, one to each coordinated concept, and the series converge at that particular point. Thus, the concept lion leads to the superior concept vertebrate, and thence unequivocally upward. Backward, however, we can pursue the concept along a different series and reach, for instance, the concept adder. Numerous other series meet in the concept animal. Thus, we can observe how even remote series, which exclude each other to begin with, meet in a single concept.

Now let us complete the previous series: lion, mammal, vertebrate, animal, living being, body, extension, space. In the concept body, an infinite number of series will converge—specifically, all those in which the principle of identity demands the exclusion of what is other than that concept. Another instance is chair, furniture, household implement, article of use, body, extension, space. If, therefore, we consider those concepts according to the principle of identity, their connection gradually brings out the concept of that principle—the concept of space. Here ends the principle of excluding all that is other than the concept.

We see how there is something common to all concepts that we are able to distinguish according to the principle of identity—the concept that corresponds precisely to that principle, the concept of space. Since, according to the principle of identity, we find the concept of space again in what is other than some particular concept, then, with the former's exclusion, the principle can cancel itself. According to the principle of identity, what is other than the concept is outside it, but now we have to deal with a conceptual relationship that bears the "other-than-the-concept" in itself. If what is "other" is taken right into the spatial concept, then we get the concept of change in space. That, however, is nothing but the concept of time relationship.

All concepts and conceptual series in which the time relationship is present as an essential part obey a form of logic in which the (spatial) contradiction rightly prevails, and the principle of identity has no validity. Here we find the starting point for a great number of antinomies. When we consider concepts and conceptual series that include time relationships as an essential element from the perspective of excluding what is other than they, contradictions arise to that viewpoint. Thus, we may encounter antinomies even when making quite elementary reflections. For instance, according to the principle of identity, it is a law that coordinated concepts are mutually exclusive; they all only include the common superordinated concept. Now if we meet with coordinated concepts that do not exclude each other, that is unlawful in terms of the principle of identity—an antinomy—and from this fact we must conclude that the principle of identity is insufficient for this case. An armchair consists of legs, a seat, the backrest, and the armrests. Those concepts are coordinated and exclude one another. Now if we assemble the coordinated concepts that contain the superordinated concept "plant," we get, roots, stalk, leaves, blossom, fruit, seed. Those concepts do not make up the plant by excluding one another, but are parts of the content that one should "grow" out of the other. Each of these concepts shows us plainly how it carries in itself what is contradictory to it—conceptually, and by no means according to the more-or-less materialistic encasement theory. The concept "seed" involves what is other than it—that is, that it should form roots and a stalk; equally is it part of the concept "stalk," that it should issue in leaves and a blossom. The contradiction in a concept, including what is other than it, is justified when we figure the time relationship as an essential part of the concept. The true concept of a seed is not that it should be equal to itself.

Now it might be said that, no matter what we introduce as part of the concept seed, it is still equal to itself in its totality. Certainly, we may say this, but then we will isolate that concept according to the spatial point of view. We will thus arrive at the common conceptual series that corresponds to the principle of identity: seed, plant, living being, body, extension, space. However, it is surely an essentially different standpoint that leads us to form this conceptual series: seed, stalk, leaf, blossom, fruit, seed... etc., a conceptual series that returns on itself. Because every link in that series includes the one following it (though relative to the superordinated concept "plant" they are coordinated), we must compare that individual grade with an entire spatial series. It is equivalent to an entire spatial series. In other words, the concept (plant) superordinated to this grade of coordinated concepts is not merely a representative of space, but by virtue of the time principle within it, it is stronger than space, so to speak. The concept plant has, for essential content, growth in space by virtue of the time principle.

Thus we reach, as a closed series of coordinated concepts, the following superordinated concepts: seed, plant, living being, growth, becoming, time. Here, too, the correctly formed conceptual series develops the underlying principle of logic, though of a higher logic that contradicts the common one. One can call it the "logic of becoming," since this concept of becoming yields the characteristic of the related concepts. The contradiction in the concept of becoming emerges most sharply for the principle of identity because it can be fulfilled only by the complete interpenetration of being and being-other. The concept of becoming demands that, at no point of the transition from the one to the other, do we conceive a jump, an incision that would enable us to say that one thing is on the one side, the other thing on the other. According to the temporal mode of viewing things, we must conceive precisely the complete unity of both—which, from the perspective of the principle of identity, is the harshest contradiction. When we wish to dissect time, which acts as the principle in becoming, we try to grasp it according to the spatial view of the principle of identity, and we are caught in contradiction. Thought must declare itself incapable of actually accomplishing the steady transition from one point of becoming to the "immediately neighboring" one, because to this end becoming would have to be split into infinitely many, infinitely neighboring points, and this could be accomplished only in an infinite time frame. This is why mathematics introduces the symbol of infinity and points to a mode of viewing things that stands fundamentally higher than that based on the principle of identity—a point of view for which the axiom of non-contradiction is not valid.

It is most interesting to see the results mathematics has reached by trying to keep itself free of any contradiction. In all of the work in this area until very recently, mathematics has unconditionally asserted the validity of the axiom of non-contradiction and, with it, the principle of identity. With regard to this, it is mainly the presuppositions of geometry that are concerned, because the elements of mathematical space must be contained in them. The so-called geometrical axioms propounded by Euclid are, according to recent investigations, essentially definitions of geometric elements; they convey what one wishes to understand by point, straight line, plane, and so on; they determine the character one attributes to the space with which geometry is concerned. This was demonstrated by the gradual abandonment of a number of those definitions or axioms. Nevertheless, it is possible to cultivate a kind of geometry that, in itself, is not less logically coherent than Euclidean geometry.

The axioms of the non-Euclidean forms of geometries contradict the Euclidean with regard to their form, because they express a contradiction relative to the corresponding Euclidean axioms. Those contradictions, however, are not important, since the contradictory propositions in each case bear no contradiction in themselves. On the contrary, they correspond with the characteristics assigned to space in any given case, and it is shown that, with sufficient practice and with the aid of any geometry, we can find our way about any of the various presupposed spaces. Now, however, in the case of all those geometries, common axioms still remain—evidently, those behind the concept of space in general.

The truly fundamental axiom is this: It is assumed that figures can be transposed unchanged in space. Such "movements" are used to prove the most important principles of geometry. Usually this axiom is expressed in three propositions: Geometrical space is a continuum; it is homogeneous and isotropic. As to the content of the geometrical theorems, the factor of time, contained in the concept "movement," plays no part in them. However, to develop that content, time is used at the beginning and then eliminated again. The fact that one must "graze" time, so to speak, to lay the foundations of spatial science can also be felt elsewhere in geometry—for instance, in all questions of continuity, which is realizable only with the aid of the concept "infinity." A straight line is a continuum—that is, it has no gaps. Its points are immediately linked to one another; two neighboring points are infinitely close. That concept can be accomplished by only thought in infinite time. Thus, time plays a peculiar part and yet remains completely outside geometry. The whole of geometry is completely surrounded, as it were, by time. That exclusion of time is expressed in the previous axiom—that a geometrical quantum is equal to itself regardless of the point in space where it is situated. This is simply our principle of identity, which also places the time concept outside itself. The principle of identity is the basic logical postulate for the science of space. Because of this, Euclidean geometry, which presupposes certain axioms not presupposed in other geometries, can be regarded as a special case of non-Euclidean geometries. By demonstrating the principle of identity and therewith of spatial logic as a special case of the logic of becoming, we can view the whole science of space as a special case of a still-unfinished science of time.

We may formulate the prime axiom of the logic of becoming: Every concept contains what is other than itself. This identity bears time within itself; it realizes itself in becoming. The concepts that correspond to this axiom are mobile; they permit us to follow all that can change in time. Nonetheless, if that change in time is nonessential, we may disregard that principle, and thus pass from the more generic to the more specific consideration. We thereby fix the concepts; we direct our gaze toward being in space. Those concepts are, of course, rigid and immobile, and we must beware of using such concepts to explain becoming. The previously cited instances of concepts are enough to illustrate this. In any case, it is clear that the kind of logic we must use depends entirely on the object of reflection. Here we leave the field of logic and again reach the epistemological fairway. Our logical reflections, however, have shown us that we must examine carefully whether a contradiction be justified. The emergence of a contradiction is not, in itself, evidence of a false inquiry.

Logic is intended to show us the relationships among thoughts; epistemology intends to show us the relationship between thinking and reality. Once we have seen that it is one-sided when thought tries to avoid all contradiction, we must illumine the question of how thinking should carry itself toward the contradictions of life and the human soul. How can we learn to distinguish when contradictions are justified or not? For this, the logical foundations of the previous chapters should be examined in relation to what follows, and in such a way that their epistemological trains of thought will be presented afresh, while the logical relationships are brought into sharper relief.

The greatest difficulty for epistemological reflections involves finding a place to begin. Because epistemology wishes to represent what forms a presupposition in all other sciences—that there is such a thing as knowledge—we must not place anything at the beginning of our epistemology that is taken from a particular science. This is generally expressed by the requirement that epistemology will be free of presuppositions. We must begin by looking more closely at the postulate "placed before" all epistemological considerations. The prohibition of presupposition is made by thinking. Therefore, if we pursue that line, we will have presupposed thought and its needs from the beginning, and if, to obviate that presupposition, we agreed not to view thought a priori as determining knowledge, we should therefore also eliminate the importance of the concept "want of presupposition." Nevertheless, that conclusion and the sentences leading up to it are likewise products of thought, as is the present statement, so that with the postulate of "no presupposition" we immediately land in a crisis of thought that turns like an endless screw.

Any beginning that we can posit will always be constructed by thought. The perception of this truth has often led to a denial of the possibility of knowledge "without presupposition," but such a denial would certainly be "illogical," since that conclusion itself is reached by thinking, as we saw in the first chapter of this section. Our assertion that every beginning must be a construct of thought, incidentally, is also a product of thought.

When thought is thus caught in its own snares, we may say that a compulsion lives in our thinking that determines the result of all our thought operations, and that is ultimately the power that bids us to strive for knowledge.

Let us, therefore, grant that power the fullest scope! We wholly eliminate ourselves and are willing not to be masters of the investigation, but await the direction in which that compulsion leads us. It is, of course, easy to interject the fact at this point that we cannot eliminate ourselves at all; even then it is still thought that does the work, that the human consciousness with its whole organization is being presupposed, and so on. Nevertheless, such arguments, as well as their refutation, merely lead us again to the endless screw. For all that, it must be pointed out that it surely makes a difference whether we have an object of thought or exclude everything from our consciousness that can be the object of thought—and further, from thought itself—all but the compulsion. We may call what then remains "pure thought"—that is, pure of all that normally fills one's consciousness. Nevertheless, pure thought is also the center of our whole consciousness and its most essential part, since it dominates the other expressions of consciousness.

Pure thought occupied us, too, in the course of our logical enquiries—that observation of thought (which concerns us in logic only as form) attains importance for epistemology with respect to content. In that coincidence of form and content, in the observation of thought, the need is manifested to speak of reality, as is argued at length in our chapter, "The 'I' and the Nature of the Human Being." In the forms constructed by logic, that compulsion operates exclusively, but those forms are, in their totality, the ultimate and determining content of our consciousness. Here we have a point where logic and epistemology meet. Because, in that chapter, the compulsion in us was left to its own devices, it was able to bring forth its own nature, and in the concept of the concept, the pure "I," the first reality resulted, which is the standard for what we may call "real." The compulsion in thought, which leads to a crisis of thought when we try to measure thought by anything else to avoid presupposing it, no longer appears to us once we give it the reins, as something foreign that acts as an external compulsion. On the contrary, we feel satisfied only when a result is born from it. We obey it gladly, because we recognize the reality of our own nature in it. Thus, viewed rightly, our own nature becomes a compulsion for us only if we sin against its reality. To be in accord with our own nature is more accurately styled freedom. Thus, the concepts receive a different value when we cause the transition from logic to epistemology. Form for logic indicates content for epistemology. "Being" is for epistemology what "thinking" is for logic. Thus, we can speak of an identity of form and content, of thinking and being.

The identity of thinking and being is knowing. If we retain the perspective of a one-sidedly specialized logic, then that identity is a contradiction. The contradiction vanishes when, in knowing, it can be posited as being, or reality. The concept of the concept is achieved for one point, the pure "I." So long as we are familiar only with the questions posed by the one-sided logic, every act of knowledge must appear as a contradiction. This is immediately clear when we consider the way in which the question of the possibility of knowledge is usually asked. A distinction is drawn there between the impression, the effect, the sensation, the mental image, and so on, produced by a thing in us and what the thing is in reality, the "thing-in-itself," whereas next it is asserted that we can surely never know what the thing-in-itself is, because we do not know if what is in our consciousness is the same thing as the thing-in-itself. This, strictly speaking, is only a requirement for what is to be called knowledge. It can be summed up as follows. The thing-for-me must be like the thing-in-itself; then knowledge is attained. If we own that requirement, we see immediately that it is satisfied in the case of the pure "I." Thus, for the preceding mode of questioning, the impossible is possible; the contradiction is knowledge. Now, however, that mode of questioning involves doubting one's own reality, and thereby thought must become entangled in the endless screw; it must speak against itself. Since, therefore, the questioning speaks against reality, when it confronts the inquiry reality must seem to the inquiry as contradiction.

In our sense, the first question of epistemology must be "What is reality?" The answer must be "I am in pure thought." Here the identity of thinking does not contradict being. If the question about reality is answered reflexively in this way, it belongs to a kind of logic that moves on a still-different plane from previously mentioned forms of logic. If all knowledge were self-knowledge or could be lifted to "I"-contemplation, we would need no other logic; there would be no contradiction. However, now life in pure thought is an exceptional condition—one we attain only when we try to penetrate to the essential epistemological question. On that path, we follow the urge for knowing, the compulsion that lives in us as reality, as pure "I," even when we operate in other areas. Our efforts toward knowledge, however, are directed not only to apprehending the pure "I," but also to knowing everything from which it has struggled upward. If this ascent occurred under the compulsion that, though it is reality, nevertheless falls short of being consciousness, descent can now take place in the consciousness of one's own reality—that is, in freedom. Thus, we may voluntarily surrender the standpoint we have gained so that we can examine how far we can speak of reality in other areas, as well. Such a surrender of the standpoint is its negation and, hence, contradiction. This contradiction will first assert itself in the "I."

We might also say that the standpoint of the pure "I" was attained by excluding what is other than "I." If we have thus unwrapped reality, this is a real process and we must concede reality, as well, to what is excluded, albeit as a reality of another plane, so to speak. It should be noted here that, through the contradistinction of the "I" and the other, or not-"I," we again adopt the perspective of the identity principle. In the ideal case previously indicated—where the pure "I" is the only area of cognition—there is nothing other than the "I." We can be clear in our own minds that, in the course of the descent, we are limiting ourselves; in any case, to the greatest degree possible we want to take the view of "I"-reality with us—that is, use contradiction as little as possible.

There is another word to be said about our means of reaching conclusions—that is, our way of linking our thoughts together. In this, we follow the mode of concluding used by common logic and, in doing so, may be certain of not going astray, quite apart from the fact that we do not yet have another at our disposal. Once we have recognized common logic as a special case of a more general one, we may feel certain that whatever holds good of the more special logic—which takes fewer liberties and therefore has more rigid laws—is certainly also valid for all more general logic. We must first try to discover the principles of a more general logic, and we may expect to do so by using normal logic as much as possible. If it fails, however, then this will point us toward a principle of a more general logic.

The first contradiction that appears when we wish to escape the "I" solitude of pure thought has to do with the "concept of the concept." We begin with that formula when we wish to determine the value and significance of any concept, since it is superordinated to all possible concepts; it is the highest peak of all that is conceptually expressible. Within its compass there is room for all possible concepts, hence, too, for those that contradict one another, even for the concept contradicting the formula itself. So long as the pure "I" is taken in its universality as pure being, or absolute reality, no concept that is in any way determined stands out.

The first differentiation appears when the pure "I" is taken as the object of knowledge, and precisely that fact is expressed in the formula, "concept of the concept." In the act of knowing itself, the "I" makes itself not-"I." Knower and known are identical in "I" knowledge; the absolute subject is at the same time its own object. The "I" is something known and is at the same time the not-"I"—the primordial contradiction that makes pure being the first object known. By confronting itself, the "I" has not yet emerged from itself, but we find that the concept of positing contains the concept of confronting, as well. The pure "I" is its own first "object" of knowledge.

The question now arises with respect to other objects of knowledge. Therefore, a second stage of contradiction begins, since what was united in the "I" must be separated. First, the union of form and content must be negated. The differentiation thus implied is carried out by the "I," in that it recognizes content in itself deriving not from itself but from the not-"I." Accordingly, in this state the "I" has negated itself as content;

it is the form for the not-"I" as content. The third stage of contradiction negates, still further, the form of the "I" and leaves it to the not-"I," so that here form and content are again united, but this time as not-"I." Here we have self-focusing of the not-"I," which has come about through triple negation of the "I." Hence, the "I" now subsists only with respect to possibility, just as we found the not-"I" subsisting in the "I" with respect to possibility. Thus, we can shape the concept of the object in three stages of contradiction. In those three stages of contradiction we must be able to find the confrontation of the "I" and the not-"I" as knowledge. If we remember that we had to ascribe reality to the totality of the not-"I," from which the "I" had detached itself, the important question now is whether our concepts, developed in three stages of contradiction, are sufficient to gain that reality as an article of knowledge.

We can recover the third stage, the self-focusing of not-"I," in what we call sensory perception, which in fact is significant only of the "I" underlying it, so that we would probably be right in calling sensory perception the part of the not-"I" that contains the "I" with respect to possibility. The second stage we may find again in the aspect of the not-"I" that lives in the "I" as sensation, mental image, feeling, instinct, and so on. However, how do we find reality in all that? We must not overlook the fact that, in the immediately posited reality of the "I" and in the reality of the not-"I" acknowledged in thought, we are faced with a contradiction. If the reality of the not-"I"—still only theoretical—is to become manifest to us, then thinking and being must also tally in relation to the unified position of "I" and not-"I." Then, the not-"I" can prove its reality in the "I"; we gain the knowledge of the not-"I." The reality of that unified position, as such, must negate the nature of the reality of the two contradictories, because as a contradiction they must be posited into one. In this connection it is important to note that no single concept showed itself as the reality of the pure "I," any more than a single sensory perception shows the reality of the not-"I." Only the totality of all possible concepts, the concept of the concept as a universal thing, is reality; likewise, we can speak only of the totality of all possible sensory perception as reality. The universality of the two contradictories must be negated when they are posited into one. The reality of the identity of the "I" and not-"I" results for cognition as individuality. In this sense, individuality is also the capacity to think and to observe the identity of the two mutually contradictory universals—"I" and not-"I."

In previous chapters, the identity of "I" and not-"I" was designated as soul, and we can now understand, with consciousness of the logical connection, how individual concepts can unite with individual sensory perceptions to form an act of cognition. Viewed from the individual soul, our human body can be defined correctly as the part of the not-"I" that is organized in terms of the "I" and the human spirit that lives in a sensing body. The condensation of the two worlds or universalities in the soul characterizes this particular stage of knowledge by the "I" knowing itself in contrast to the not-"I." The pure thoughts of the "I" can converge with the pure sensory perceptions of the not-"I" in the soul as knowing. The basic character of that stage of knowledge is "this-beside-that," the determination of phenomena in space. From the perspective of the pure "I," that knowledge has, to begin with, three stages of contradiction; in other words, starting from the pure "I," we had to pace off three stages of contradiction to find things in space. Thus, we see how contradiction is highly significant for the genesis of our knowledge; contradiction can be our guide through the stages of reality. The chapter "Natural Science and Spiritual Science" showed how we can take our bearings with respect to things in space; it is easily shown how we can characterize that way from the perspective of the philosophy of contradiction.

First, we find the things in space that express, through their qualities, precisely the essence of space, and the "rigid" logic of identity may be applied to them. They exclude what is other than themselves; they remain unchanged of themselves. We call them three-dimensional because they express three stages of contradiction to us, and this is why we represent the three dimensions of space as positioned at right angles to one another. They are the minerals. In the sciences that deal with the mineral realm, we continually encounter the three dimensions, or three stages, of contradiction, which are used unconsciously as the basis of all mineral (physical, chemical, etc.) knowledge. We find them expressed most definitely in the basic concepts of physics.

The science concerning the nature of "force" corresponds to the first dimension. Its geometrical symbol is the straight line. If we add to a force another, equally great and opposed to it (contradictory), we obtain what physics calls a "state." All phenomena of "tension" are two-dimensional; its geometrical symbol is the plane. Things in the mineral realm pose a resistance to all the phenomena of tension; its expression is the concept of "mass," which appears as the third dimension. Its geometrical symbol is the solid. More generally, in the case of a mineral being that we contemplate in space, we can say, too, that we must inquire about the forces that act upon it (first dimension), about the forces in equilibrium with it (second dimension), and about the forces that emanate from it (third dimension). In this sense, we can speak of mineral phenomena as of a sum of forces.

Now we encounter beings in space that show still other kinds of forces, different from those of the three dimensions. The next type of force contradicts the mineral forces, as was demonstrated in the chapter mentioned. We designate the beings that directly contradict the mineral forces as plants. If we would comprehend that contradiction in knowledge, we must consider it an expression of a reality. The plant directs us beyond the three stages of space toward the fourth stage, or dimension, of contradiction. To know the plant in space, we must concede a place in our thought to that contradiction. This is done by recognizing how the plant contradicts the mineral realm—that is, by means of time, which to the mineral is still something extraneous. We can say, "The plant overcomes space through time." The logic of the principle of identity cannot be applied to the plant's nature; here is the place for logic that contradicts the three-dimensional logic, a logic of becoming, or time.

Again, we have to deal with new forces in the case of the animal kingdom. These forces contradict the mineral and plant forces. The animal detaches itself from the mother soil without perishing, as the plant does when detached from its soil. The animal, accordingly, points us toward a fifth stage of contradiction, a fifth dimension. To comprehend the animal in space, we must incorporate that new contradiction into our thinking. We can do this by recognizing what is still extraneous even to the plant as essential to the animal. The animal's form of reality in space asserts itself by the fact that, having become detached from the mother soil, the animal displays forces of inwardness through perception and activity. The animal lives in accordance with motives. The essential thing thus indicated is correctly called causality, a principle inward to the animal. The animal overcomes time and space through causality. Thus, we can call the animal a five-dimensional being in the same sense that the plant is a four-dimensional one. The new contradiction that we must incorporate with our thought is shown by this—that when dealing with the animal, even the concepts of becoming no longer suffice us. We need a kind of logic of inwardness, of causality (psychology). Thus, we can propound the following axioms:

Logic of the three dimensions:

> Every concept excludes what is other than it. Logic of the four dimensions:
> Every concept includes what is other than it. Logic of the five dimensions:
> Every concept acts by what is other than it.

The three-dimensional beings point us toward the concept of the "this-beside-that"; the four-dimensional, toward that of the "one-after-another"; the fifth-dimensional ones, toward that of "this-because-that."

Thus, we return again to the human being, who represents a new, sixth stage of contradiction. Human beings must overcome their animal nature, must contradict it, to be human. Only thus can we achieve self-awareness. In the knowledge of self-awareness, human beings makes themselves masters of space, time, and causality by being able, in freedom, to place their own goals and destinies before themselves. In self-awareness, the concept becomes immediate reality. If logic can still be spoken of here, its basic axiom must be "The 'I' creates itself from what is other." The human being appears in space as a six-dimensional being. In the human being, the creative force that appears as "dimensions" in the other beings in space grows conscious of itself. Now human beings must strive beyond themselves for self-fulfillment as creative beings. Immediate creative force can be designated the seventh dimension, but as the culmination of contradiction, it is also undimensionality, possibility, and source of appearance. Up to this point, the principle of contradiction leads us in the knowledge of the beings in space. This is where philosophy ends and Anthroposophy begins.

~

Now we must summarize. When our thinking drove us into an endless screw, we abandoned ourselves to the compulsion in our thought; it led us to the reality of the "I." The nature of that reality was found in contradiction, and so we delivered our thinking over to contradiction and allowed it to lead us. Contradiction showed us how human beings confront with their consciousness objects in space. The various stages of contradiction that we had to accomplish in thought oriented us with regard to the beings in space. They showed us tokens of the true reality of the beings in nature, but we were unable to grasp that true reality itself. What we subsequently designated as reality and knowledge is not yet true reality. We see that, as a result, the path along which contradiction led us through the realms of nature showed us only the pure "I" as a self-contained being. To our perception and thinking in space, the beings of nature and human beings, insofar as they are not pure "I," appear as illusion, or maya. However, we can also see that, in fact, a higher consciousness is needed for us to apprehend the true reality of the world. Anthroposophy would show us the path toward that goal.

In the sense of our terminology, we can say that, as human beings, we live as a reality in space when we can apprehend our own "I" as the sixth stage of contradiction. That sixth stage of contradiction—as the reality of the "I"—was active in our consideration. It led us to understand the tokens of the true reality of beings in nature as projections into three dimensions. We can become conscious of this true reality only by recognizing ourselves as six-dimensional beings, in contrast to the other beings in space. Now, if we can also grasp the other beings in their sixth stage of contradiction, the "I"-stage, then we have found their true reality. It is true that the human being in space possesses six dimensions; we can grasp them in thought and experience them in the pure "I," but our ordinary consciousness attains only three dimensions. Through them, we place ourselves in contrast to things. Anthroposophy, on the other hand, wishes to lift us through our consciousness to the higher dimensions, which it does by incorporating contradiction as a reality—not merely in theory, with the three-dimensional consciousness that places human beings over against things. We must learn to sacrifice three-dimensional consciousness.

The effect described to us by the spiritual investigator suggests that consciousness gradually penetrates to the heart of things and no longer stands in contrast to them. That is true, living contradiction compared to three-dimensional consciousness. The results of spiritual investigation come about as a direct result of the reality of contradiction. If we penetrate to the heart of things in this way, we can become acquainted with their true reality, just as in three-dimensional consciousness we can know only our "I." Anthroposophy shows us three stages of a higher reality, and therefore three stages of the reality of contradiction. These are the three higher worlds: the astral and the lower and upper devachan.

Thus we approach the nature of Spiritual Science, or Anthroposophy, from a new angle. It takes contradiction, in fact, seriously. As a result of our reflections, we are provided with at least the possibility of grasping important areas of anthroposophic teaching and, above all, what they have to say about the true reality of natural beings. If we apply our three-dimensional consciousness and the three stages of contradiction in the ordinary logic, we can follow the expressions of mineral beings in space. If we now take up contradiction in thought, or logic, step by step, we can follow the expressions of the true reality of plants and animals in space. We finally reach human beings who, in accordance with their nature, show themselves as true reality already in space.

Now, however, it is something far more different when those who push forward to the sources of Anthroposophy in truth allow contradiction, step by step, into the reality of the "I." We thus unfold our higher nature and attain knowledge of the astral and the lower and higher devachanic worlds. We find true human reality when we pace off the six stages of contradiction and remain in space. To find the true reality of the mineral phenomenon, we must look for it at the sixth stage of contradiction, the "I" stage. We find three stages of contradiction for the mineral in space and must yet pace off three more stages—that is, through the astral and lower devachanic into the upper devachanic world, where the spiritual investigator finds the "I" of the mineral thing. A plant displays four stages of contradiction in space; hence, the sixth stage, the true reality, must be found in the lower devachanic world. The animal, which displays five stages of contradiction in space, needs but one more stage of contradiction up to the astral world to find its true reality.

We can apply the usual designations to the several stages of contradiction:

Three stages of contradiction: Physical body. (1)
Four stages of contradiciton: Etheric body. (2)
Five stages of contradiction: Astral body. (3)
Six stages of contradiction: "I." (4)

Now, where the several members of the natural beings are to be sought emerges in a simple way, and we get the familiar classification:

	Physical world	Astral world	Lower devachan	Upper devachan
Mineral	(1)	(2)	(3)	(4)
Plant	(1) (2)	(3)	(4)	
Animal	(1) (2) (3)	(4)		
Human	(1) (2) (3) (4)			

This works out like a simple sum in arithmetic, and we can grasp it with the help of our reflections. As spiritual investigators, it comes as immediate knowledge when we explore the higher worlds in which we find the true reality of what projects itself for us in the three-dimensional consciousness in a world of maya, as space, time, and causality. However, if we learn to find our own natures as true reality, then this is a sign to us that all the beings of nature, too, speak their higher dimensions into our world. To thoughtful contemplation, the members of the natural beings that send out their influence from the higher worlds bear clear marks of their origin, and artistic feeling may show us the nature of that influence. The artistic outlook on life loses nothing if we can interpret in their beauty the colors and forms that appeal to our senses as expressions of spiritual influences.

In this way, the contradictions of life and the soul can become for us expressions of a higher reality, and the admission of the reality of contradiction is to show us the path to the higher worlds. We will have to leave for another presentation the consequences to human life that arise from the nature of contradiction.

~

Wherever true reality acts on our consciousness, it appears as contradiction; it comes powerfully down into our lives from the higher worlds. We must strive freely to incorporate it into our true being; otherwise, it acts as an external power. We must learn to sacrifice our ordinary consciousness to fulfill the meaning of human becoming. The sway of the higher worlds, whose last creative act is the human "I," even as it is at the same time the first creative act of humankind, does not allow the "I" to grow rigid in "being," and places death in the midst of life as the strongest expression of the true reality found only in the higher worlds. We can understand that death is the true reality of life. Thus, also for human life, true reality signifies the death at the center of its becoming: the death on Golgotha.

www.ingramcontent.com/pod-product-compliance
Lightning Source LLC
Chambersburg PA
CBHW022111090426
42743CB00008B/810